A DOORWAY TO THE LIGHT

A DOORWAY TO THE LIGHT

After
Death
Experiences

Carmen de Sayve &
Jocelyn Arellano

www.whitecrowbooks.com

Published by White Crow Books, an imprint of White Crow Productions Ltd.

A CIP catalogue record for this book is available from the British Library.

For information, contact White Crow Books by
e-mail: info@whitecrowbooks.com.

Cover Design by Astrid@Astridpaints.com
Interior design by Velin@Perseus-Design.com

Paperback: ISBN: 978-1-78677-268-8
eBook: ISBN: 978-1-78677-269-5

NON-FICTION / Afterlife & Reincarnation

www.whitecrowbooks.com

Contents

~

Preface

~

We are living in a crucial stage in the history of mankind, a critical era where advances in science and technology have provided humanity with a series of advantages that previous generations could never have even conceived—but on the same token—have engendered a wide range of conflicts and peril. Pressed by preoccupation and angst, the sign of our times, we human beings are rediscovering a most ancient source of guidance and help: that which derives from the ability to establish communication with the spiritual world, whether it be angels, saints, or simply departed loved ones, who from another realm of reality, continue to provide us with their protection and support. While these practices, considered clairvoyance, have always existed, in recent years there seems to have been an awakening of a growing number of people to the ability of establishing themselves as a bridge and connection to the "beyond." *A Doorway to the Light*, by Carmen de Sayve and Jocelyn Arellano, is a clear example of just that. It includes a series of impressive testimonials that tell of the challenges faced by souls unable to move towards the light, who are trapped in the so-called lower astral plane. As we continue reading, we learn of the causes that lead to such a deplorable condition—materialism, arrogance, egoism, addictions—and the how we can contribute to liberating those souls.

Throughout the book, the reader will perceive and intuit the realism and veracity of these stories. It is evident that the writers have been able to effectively convey the voices and images sourced in other dimensions, that they have captured through their extensive experience in dealing with all types of spirits.

There are books that transform us to the extent that they change our mindset. This is a book of that sort. For that reason, no doubt it will provide a great many people with a broader, better understanding of what life after death is, and it will also serve as a useful guide in aiding those who, after passing on, are immersed in darkness, enabling them to receive support from higher beings that already reside in the light.

My sincere gratitude goes to Carmen de Sayve and Jocelyn Arellano for their most original, interesting and enlightening work.

Antonio Velasco Piña

Introduction

∼

He who teaches men how to die,
Teaches them how to live.
~Montaigne

Throughout time, humankind has wondered whether death means the total annihilation of our being, or if there could be life after death; and, if life does continue, where does it lead? All religions and schools of philosophy have their theories on the subject, and while many reject the possibility of immortality, many others believe in the persistence of the soul.

Undoubtedly, death is a mystery. The lone certainty is that we will all sooner or later go through this process called death, which, ironically, is the one thing we are least prepared for. Given that death is inevitable for everyone born into the physical realm, perhaps we would be wise to understand it more and so fear it less.

The concept of death seems to present us with either eternity or nothingness. There have been attempts to prove or disprove both, both by scientific and philosophical means. However, it's a fallacy to believe that one can do this scientifically, as science corresponds to the rational mind and the world of the senses, while disincarnate life corresponds to another system of reality, one composed of far subtler vibrations. How can we hope to measure the intangible with an instrument limited to the tangible? No wonder the afterlife has yet to be scientifically accepted. Yet, there is increasing evidence to suggest its existence. In various countries, experiments have yielded surprising results, including recorded voices of the so-called dead, even entire conversations, using devices developed specifically for this purpose, as well as startling video images.

The purpose of this book is not to demonstrate what each of us already believes or disbelieves. It is solely to communicate knowledge derived directly from other realities, or based on studies in related fields, and to share a series of first-hand experiences that could only have originated in other levels of consciousness—and to draw from a truth that becomes more evident each day: that human consciousness indeed survives the disintegration of the physical body.

Because of our fear of death, we ignore it, try not to think about it, and reject it as an enemy of life. Especially for materialists, death signifies the absolute end, for the disintegration of the body and the brain means the intelligence it contains also ceases to be. Actually, the brain is but an instrument that the mind uses to express itself within this dimension. The reality is, life is eternal and our human lives are no more than a small part of a far greater existence, of a process of evolution in which we all participate. We are not limited to a single journey on earth but rather a grand evolutionary process toward perfection.

In recent years, there have been increasing reports of people declared clinically dead yet returning to life. Drs. Raymond Moody, Melvin Morse, and Kenneth Ring, among others, have compiled many accounts of experiences with astonishing similarities and fascinating facts about the threshold of death. These reports show that, upon clinical death, an individual leaves the physical body then observes it from a different reality. This is followed by a passage through a tunnel toward a marvelous light, from which emanates a feeling of indescribable peace and love. The sense of freedom and joy people experience in this threshold state overrides any desire to return to earthly existence, but for various reasons, something impels them to re-enter the physical vessel.

All those who experience the threshold of death and return, go through a radical transformation in their lives. Fear of death disappears giving way to an awareness of the true meaning of life. One realizes that the most important thing is to act from the standpoint of LOVE. The experience of another dimension, ironically, brings us closer to the true meaning of earthly life, which is one of learning and evolution.

These experiences prove that our consciousness is independent of the physical body and persists after its death.

Though we are taught to deny death and fear even its mention, dying is an integral part of living, and the more we reject it, the more difficult will be the moment of our transition and even after. It is fear itself that keeps us from experiencing both life and death to their fullest: fear of changes in our daily lives, fear of the judgments of others, fear of not being recognized, fear of leaving behind what we have gathered, and fear of the unknown, of the end. The sooner we understand that life is a process of continual evolutionary change, the better we will be able to accept the approach of death. Actually, we must continually die to the past in order to live and learn from what life offers us in the present. The more we see death as, not the end of our existence, but a doorway to a greater reality, and the more we are able to familiarize ourselves with death, the freer we will be from needless fears.

When we say that nothing lasts and everything changes, we mean that the seeming permanence of this world is illusory, and that the only thing real and everlasting is the higher self, or divine essence. Physical bodies and various experiences come and go, but spirit is eternal. If only we could take the news of someone's death as an opportunity to celebrate the transitory nature of all except our most defining truth.

Neither the universe nor anything in it, is static. All is in perpetual flux, and death is inevitable. Why not welcome this moment calmly, knowing that, in the long journey of evolution, there is still much to discover? Another life awaits, one that too will seem "real."

We are afraid of the unknown, but our greatest fear is the unknown in ourselves. When we see ourselves as separate from creation, we lose sight of our identity and feel alone and vulnerable. We base our sense of security and identity on external things that vanish at the time of death. We spend our lives trying to affirm who we are through control of our own lives and those of others. This is the reason behind our fear: losing everything that we have based our identity on, though those things were, in fact, nothing but illusion. They were illusory in the sense that what we believed in so literally, was actually a theatrical scene in which we participated in order to learn and grow. When the curtain comes down for each of us, we return to our true essence, and the meaning of the script becomes clear.

We wish to convey to our readers certain experiences that have allowed us entry into other dimensions of living where we have encountered the so-called dead. We'd like to share how those encounters have helped us to better understand the difficulties that many souls endure before freeing themselves of old attachments to earthly life. Once free, those souls transition to the realm of light most appropriate for them. We have come to understand that the ease or difficulty of this transition is based on each person's spirituality.

We all have psychic abilities, or channeling abilities, though in some individuals these gifts are more developed than in others. Without realizing it, we are all in continuous contact with other dimensions where the supposed dead reside—who in reality are more alive than we. They are always helping us, whether we call them saints, masters, guides, guardian angels, or know them simply as family members who have passed on. All are interested in our wellbeing and evolution, and they communicate with us by telepathic means. How often have we avoided a dangerous situation, or resolved an important issue in our lives, by following a gut feeling or a thought that seemed to have come from nowhere? We not only receive help from the unseen others; we can help them, as well. This is the meaning of "the communion of saints."

It was in a meditation and prayer circle that we first made contact with departed souls in need of our help. They came to us, just as unsolicited teachings have come to us, rather than we to them, by way of Carmen's intuitive writing. We wish to be clear that we've never sought out communication with souls in transition; rather, they have presented themselves to us for guidance.

We do not claim that these pages contain the final truth concerning the various processes of death. The experiences we relate, and the teachings they convey, have come to us directly through the time-honored practice of mediumship (channeling), or else by way of ancillary studies. It is important to know that, just as a fish flows through water and comes out wet, messages through a medium can sometimes be influenced by his or her subconscious. A medium, or psychic, is an intermediary who bridges two realities, one of these realities being unknown, there may be errors in reception or interpretation. That said, this book is the result of a meticulous process of discernment that cross-references a variety of sources. Those sources generally corroborate the messages we have received. Still, the reader should trust his or her own critical faculties and intuition, and so form his or her own conclusions.

Upon leaving the physical world and arriving in the astral, the mind may be conflicted by deep attachments to the lower vibrations of earth. In its natural form, the soul is attracted to the light. However, the call of what it has just left behind, its rebellion against accepting its new condition, its sense of guilt, its arrogance in feeling spiritually superior and not finding what it expected, or the non-believer who expects nothing at all, are some of the reasons why certain souls find themselves caught in a limbo that can be difficult to escape.

Preparing ourselves for death is much the same as preparing ourselves for life. In either case, we must first understand our true essence and the purpose of our existence. The problem is that, once we have taken material form, we quickly forget our divine origin and circumscribe ourselves with the limitations of the physical world. Increasingly ignorant of our true identity, our minds focus solely on the physical, making little use of our true powers. In order to escape this self-fashioned trap, we must reclaim our awareness of the One whom we collectively are. This return to our "right mind" gives us the power to create more harmonious worlds and realities while still in the body. One way to achieve this return is through meditation, which encourages a healthy detachment from worldly problems and pleasures that can hold our hearts prisoner.

Dying is a lot easier than being born. While the former is liberating, the latter is limiting. In one, we return home, while in the other we enroll in the difficult school of earthly life. As long as we fail to see both life and death as part of something larger, we will struggle with death, which is, in reality, a joyous graduation from a rigorous school. To live life fully is to live fully conscious of death.

Death—feared by many, contemplated by others, but destined for all—is not the end of life but a transition from one state to another, from one form of life to another. Life is a divine gift with no beginning and no end. We are as eternal as the energy source from which we all come, whom we refer to as God. From Him we arise, and to Him we shall return.

1

Death Does Not Exist

~

If you love me, do not weep.
If only you knew the gift of God
And what heaven is!
If only you could hear the angels sing
And see me among them!
If only you could contemplate for one moment
The beauty that I see,
And before which all others fall and fade!
You who have loved me
In the land of shadows,
Why are you not resigned to see me
In the land of immutable realities?
Believe me, when on that day chosen by God,
Your soul reaches heaven where I have preceded you,
Then you will see He who has always loved you
And you will find his heart with tenderness purified,
Transfigured, joyful,
No longer waiting for death,
But ever hand in hand with you,
Walking in the paths of light.
Wipe away your tears
And, if you love me, weep no more.
~ Saint Augustine

In reality, nothing dies, for the truth of what we are is unchanging. The body is simply a costume that we wear for a while to express in physical reality. Once it is no longer of use, when its purpose is complete, it returns to the earthly elements from which it rose. The body is no more than an instrument, as illusory as is the rest of the three-dimensional world. As it lacks reality, the body cannot really "live" or "die." What does have life here is consciousness, which can never die. At the moment of physical death, it simply leaves its temporary abode and withdraws to another plane, one far more real than the physical world. That which truly lives, lives forever. Death then is rebirth in another vibrational frequency.

Although many religions believe in the persistence of the soul and claim that man's identity is separate from his physicality, those religions express little interest in documented cases of communication with the dead. Such communication is called Spiritism and tends to be viewed with skepticism, as some so-called spiritists have been revealed as frauds. This is the equivalent of dismissing science because of a few unreliable scientists.

Throughout this work, we will relate certain experiences the authors have had with souls who'd lost their way following separation from the physical body. Some such communications occurred spontaneously during the course of weekly group meditations. During those meditation sessions, the departed sometimes spoke through one of the participants with highly developed channeling abilities. The information was then corroborated by Carmen by way of her intuitive writing. This was done "blind," that is, without either participant knowing what the other was receiving.

Although such work is certainly not easy due to our unsure footing in unknown realms, we have done our best to help the souls who present themselves to us, as they seem to be caught in a limbo between the physical and the spiritual.

We rely on the aid of unseen masters and guides to facilitate the encounter as we offer assistance and comfort to those in need, both the disembodied and their remaining family members. We have also been asked to counsel people near death, that they might have a smooth transition. All such work might seem haphazard, in that scientific instruments are unable to prove its veracity, but Carmen and I are increasingly convinced that coincidences do not exist. That which is needed comes forward in response to our willingness to help.

What we do, in accord with our spiritual helpers, is offer ourselves as instruments to help those caught in the lower reaches of the astral, or spiritual, world. Because those souls are still very near earthly frequencies, they can receive our communications quite readily. The essential difference between our work and that of spiritists, is that spiritualists initiate contact with the departed in order to clarify worldly issues; We, on the other hand, respond to requests for assistance in helping them access the spiritual plane where they belong. Why do they require our help? In many cases, the problem is a continuing preoccupation with earthly matters. If the departed continues to resonate with the familiar earthly frequency, he or she is unable to rise to a more expanded state of being. Spiritists run the risk of invoking souls no longer present in the lower astral plane. Though a disincarnate entity may reply to such invocations, it may be an impersonator, someone of a very low vibrational frequency with nothing better to do than fool us into believing we're contacting a departed loved one. This can result in an unhealthy obsession among grieving family members, one that may lead to extremely negative situations. For this reason, we never seek to contact a specific soul but instead make ourselves available to any who request our aid, and always under the protection of our guides.

The following cases illustrate some common reasons why a soul might remain stuck in the lower astral rather than advancing toward the light. Many cultures liken the journey after death to crossing a river, or passing through a tunnel, or some other passage from one place to another, from a familiar reality to one completely different. This passage signifies the vibrational change required for a newly disembodied soul to reach the spiritual realms. A successful transition depends on the vibrational frequencies of the mind. Those who cannot, or will not, cross over are still tuned to the frequency of the material world, rather than the light beckoning from the world of spirit. In many cases, they do not realize that they are dead. In others, they are afraid of the punishment they've been told awaits them. Some are disoriented because they died expecting to encounter oblivion. Some are distraught due to strong attachments to their loved ones, or work, or belongings. These and other factors can keep us from seeing and accepting the light.

The following testimonies illustrate such difficulties as these. Each demonstrates that penance does not exist, nor does punishment, but we may encounter the results of our own beliefs, however inaccurate. Happily, thought we are all protected by God's boundless compassion for his children, whom he takes under his wing with infinite love.

The cases discussed here are actual. Only names and other identifying details have been changed, in order to protect the privacy of those involved.

There are times when death occurs so suddenly or violently that the people involved do not initially realize they are dead. They don't understand what has happened to them, so in a sense they are still alive, only no one can see them, nor are they able to communicate with their loved ones. This feeling can be very disturbing, as the following example shows.

I Have No Body, Yet I'm Alive

Sister Lucia is an old acquaintance. She is a generous woman, a nun dedicated to volunteer work in a working-class neighborhood. Sister Lucia was an attendee in our meditation course as part of her spiritual search. One day, I received a call from Sister Lucia, who sounded very distressed. She asked to see me immediately concerning a problem.

"This isn't about me, Jocelyn," said Sister Lucia. "There's a girl named Paula, a very distressed young girl who has asked for my help. She feels ... no, she doesn't just feel ... she actually sees a presence in her home; a man who follows her and harasses her. Sometimes it seems that he wants to rape her. Paula doesn't understand. She thinks it's her fault, that it's some kind of punishment for something she has done. Her family doesn't believe her. They tell her she's crazy, and the poor girl no longer knows if what she's seeing is real, or if she's losing her mind. I have to help her somehow, Jocelyn. I think you ... please, just come with me to see her."

I spoke with Carmen about the matter, and we decided to accompany Sister Lucia to Paula's house to see if there was anything we could do.

The road snaked up a forested hill, and the three of us left the city far below in a cloud of smog. We drove down a street lined with humble houses.

"Here it is." Sister Lucia pointed to an alley at whose end was a blue door with chipped paint.

We crossed a dirt yard and passed through bed sheets and clothes that had been hung out to dry. A young girl came out to invite us in. She walked with her head down, face partially covered by long black hair.

We entered a poorly furnished room. There was nothing to see but a few chairs and a table, and nothing to hear but the cry of a small child from what seemed the only bedroom. Taking a seat, Paula related what she had been going through, often hesitating with what seemed fear and distrust. Since the day she had moved into this house with her family, she had been having what she called visions. She often caught glimpses of a strong, dark young man intent on harassing her. Paula could feel an unaccountable aggressiveness from him that filled her with fear. Though he seemed to have no physical body, Paula sometimes feared that he would rape her, such was the hatred that came from him.

"Do you see him at school," we asked, "or on the street, or anywhere else besides your house?"

"Never. It's always here."

We lit candles on the table, and their light shined brightly on the plastic tablecloth, and the smoke of incense wafted around us.

We asked Sister Lucia to pray, and suggested that she concentrate on the word *love* and on sending a pink light to the disincarnate being we had come to help. We asked Paula to do the same. The pale girl sat very close to the nun and closed her eyes. Carmen and I, meanwhile, concentrated on achieving a meditative state. Little by little, the pen that Carmen held over a piece of paper began to move. A telepathic transmission confirmed the presence of the disembodied being Paula had been sensing:

> *I find myself in my house, but there are other people living here, too, and this makes me furious. I don't know what has happened to me. I was fighting with some guys, and when I woke up, I realized something had changed. Ever since then, no one hears me, and it's driving me crazy. Only this child, Paula, can see me, but she's afraid of me.*

We answered him, "What has happened is that you are dead to this plane. You don't belong here anymore. You need to leave this place and go toward the light, where awaits a life filled with love and peace. We're now sending you loving energy, which will help you to understand."

Again, the pen wrote:

I see some kind of light surrounding you, but all around is a terrible darkness. How am I supposed to feel your love when I have never felt love for anyone? When you speak, though, I do feel a sense of wellbeing.

"The wellbeing you feel is nothing compared to what awaits if you leave this prison and go toward God. All you have to do is ask."

I don't understand what you're saying. I don't even believe in God.

"As you can see," we replied, "you no longer have a body, so you can't manifest on this level anymore. Your life has to continue elsewhere. Death does not exist, but only steps along a path of evolution toward true life. A wonderful life is awaiting you, if only you will accept it."

I know that I have no body, yet I'm alive. How right you are that death does not exist, though I believed it to. It is a terrible thing, but existence has no end.

"What is your name?" we asked.

Rodolfo. I don't know what's happening to me.

"You feel confused because you still want to be here, but your new state of being won't allow it. Your confusion is due to your denying your new reality. That's what is keeping you here in the darkness. The light is there, and if you call to it, you will begin to feel a sense of wellbeing. You will be greeted by beings of light who will take you where you belong, to a life of love, peace, and harmony."

I can see your light, the light that surrounds you, but nothing else. You tell me to call for the light. But who's listening? You say very beautiful things, and I'd like to believe them.

We concentrated on sending Rodolfo light, surrounding him with loving energy.

"Ask God to help you out of your confusion, and beg for the light to be shown to you. His compassion and love are infinite. He only waits for you to open to Him."

Another message appeared on the paper:

I can see glimpses of light, but I don't know where they come from. Your words give me great peace. Each time I look, I can see a little more light, and I think I believe you. I'm moving toward the light, and it's becoming brighter.

"Allow yourself to move toward the light," we urged. We continued to pray and send harmonious energy to help this soul find release.

Yes, yes. It's marvelous. Keep helping me. I think I'm finally getting free from this glue that has had me trapped. How did I not see this before? I feel lighter, like I'm free of a great weight, and I think I now see the beings of light calling to me. I can truthfully say that I feel joy. Thank you, whoever you are, and I ask Paula's pardon. I won't bother her anymore. I'm going to heaven.

The reason why Paula could see him, but not the others in her family, is that she is psychically sensitive. We later learned that the young man who had lived in the house had been killed in a fight nearby. We also learned that after our session, Paula never saw him again, and peace returned to her home. Cases such as this demonstrate how souls sometimes do not realize they are dead and try to continue to participate in this realm.

Other times, people's values extend only to material things, and so they remain attached to them, as we will see in the following case.

I Thought Death Was Total Annihilation

The studio is always bathed in light, not only from the large windows, but from Isabel's canvases, as well. Mountains, lakes, the cold light from the Scandinavian sun, form subtle geometries that tell of a clear yet fantastic universe. But it has not always been like this.

After her friend Camilla's death, Isabel felt something in the studio that they had shared for so long. It was a presence of some kind, a shift in the atmosphere of the space that had once felt so familiar. Isabel's artwork reflected this shift that only she could feel. She found herself in a period of great productivity, but the theme of her work seemed to have changed. The paintings came with incredible ease. But, since Camilla's death, unseen landscapes would appear in her mind as clearly as the sun that shone down on the meadows, now transformed into negative messages. Oftentimes, surprised by her own creations, she would search through books for the images that appeared in her paintings and discover very similar ones in witchcraft. From what dark world did these unrecognizable images emerge and, as if by their own will, appear in her creations? Worried,

Isabel called us. Something or someone she could not identify was constantly interrupting her work to dictate mysterious visions. Intelligent and skeptical, Isabel refused to consider the possibility of paranormal activity. Her life was ruled by logic and reason, and she couldn't comprehend a force beyond her control. Nevertheless, she thought of us, as her days were tainted by an inexplicable fear that interrupted her work that had once brought great satisfaction.

We found Isabel in her studio. The atmosphere, though not actually dark, felt cold and heavy. We began our ritual as usual with Gregorian chants and vases of white flowers among the many paintbrushes and tubes of paint. The light aroma of the flowers blended with the acrid smell of oil and solvents in the air. Carmen had brought long, thin candles, and we lit these, along with sticks of incense.

The three of us sat around the table, and Carmen's pen began to move:

They tell me that I no longer belong in this place, but what other place is there? I'm not dead, as I expected to be. I'm still alive, yet I can't do things on my own. Isabel does them for me, and very well. This power that I have over her is very interesting.

We responded, "You have to continue your process of evolution in another place, one much better than this one. You are still attached to your work, and this is why you believe there is no other place. You're mentally influencing your friend and this fascinates you. But, as you have realized, you cannot do things on your own, and this proves that you must accept your new reality and so see the beautiful world that awaits you; a new life filled with love and harmony. You only have to wish to leave behind this state in which you find yourself, and call upon the light."

How do I know that what you say exists? You're saying things that I have never heard of and do not believe. Saying that all I have to do is call for the light, is very easy. That's just witchcraft, and I don't believe in it. Why is it that I don't see a light, and yet I do see a certain luminosity when you speak and when you say the word love?

"We are sending you thoughts of love," we replied. "This is why you see light surrounding us. It is all energy, and what you perceive is the energy of our thoughts. The more love they carry, the more light you perceive. Death does not exist. Rather, there is a doorway to true life and continuing ascension. All human beings are in a process of spiritual growth, which we accomplish by letting go and accepting the reality of our situation. In order for you to perceive the light, the love, and the peace that await you, you must humbly accept that your place is no longer here and open your mind to new realities. You must simply wish to see the light."

You are telling me things I have never believed, but now I am beginning to waver. I thought death was total annihilation, but now I see that it's not so. I do feel great tranquility when you speak, but I want to continue to create art and beauty, and if I go to the other side I will no longer be able to. (At that moment, the cat in the studio emitted a long meow.) *See, this spirit crying for me is the only one who accompanies me in my solitude, and the only one who can see me.*

"You will create much beauty if you let yourself be taken where you belong. You must trust what has happened to you and give in to divine will. The creating that you speak of is nothing compared to what you will create in the magnificent realms that await you."

You say that I no longer belong here. That's hard for me to believe. I will think about it, though, and we will speak again.

We focused on sending Camilla harmonious energy and told her that, if she would move toward the light, the pleasant feelings would intensify.

I do not understand what you are giving me. True, it is very pleasant, but it is difficult to believe that this is what I will feel if I leave this place. Either way, thank you for your positive intentions. We'll talk later.

A week later, we returned to speak with Camilla again, and she was ready to talk:

Good afternoon, dear friends. I have been reflecting on what you've said, and I am not convinced. I do not feel happy here, it's true. But was I even happy during my time on earth?

"Happiness is not a place," we replied. "It is a state of consciousness. You were not happy on earth, nor are you happy now because you are still attached to your ego. It is your ego who feels that happiness depends on something external to yourself."

You say that neither this place nor earth are happiness. Then where is it?

"You cannot find happiness because you're still attached to what you have left behind. Happiness is accepting life as it presents itself to you; it is acting from love rather than from ego."

I am separated from everything that I enjoy and love. How can you expect me to be happy?

"The things you loved were there for you when you needed them. Their time is over, and you don't need them anymore. Leave those thoughts behind for a moment and call for the light. Do you see the light we're sending you?"

I do see it. It is the only light I see. And when you speak, I see a splendorous luminescence of some kind.

"That is the light of the Creator, who is in all that exists. We all come from Him, and to Him we must return. Allow yourself to be drawn to that light which is love, peace, harmony and beauty."

You say there is a Creator, but I don't see Him, nor do I believe He exists. Only fools believe there's a supreme being.

"Everything could not have come from nothing. Look at the marvelous structure of the human body. It had to have been conceived by a superior intelligence to work the way it does."

You could almost convince me with this argument. The human body is, in fact, magnificent. Yet, it has one great flaw. It doesn't last forever.

We explained that the body is simply an instrument that we use for the work that we do in this world, but now new experiences await her, much more interesting ones that will allow her creativity to expand to unimaginable heights.

You're making me hope for something I cannot believe, but if you want me to call for the light, I'm willing to try.

"Call for it. Ask God to help you."

I'd really like to believe you. There is a lot of darkness where I am, and no light at all. I need to see light. Give me the strength to overcome my pride.

We continued to tell Camellia to seek the light. Meanwhile, we were mentally sending light to her. We prayed, as well, because prayer has an energy that helps the poor souls attached to a place where they no longer belong, lifting them and releasing them from this plane of existence.

I feel something when you speak. Give me strength. I am starting to see the light you speak of. When I see it, I feel warmth and wellbeing.... This is given to any who call for it with all their hearts.... I'm going toward the light, and I feel lighter.... You give me strength to go on.... Thank you. I can see beings reaching out to me, and as I walk toward them I feel a sense of wellbeing. ... Goodbye, dear Isabel. It's no longer worth it to remain here. I think our friends are right. Your prayers have helped me. I understand the process now. Goodbye, and continue to send me help.

Creation and Illusory World

To understand the process of death, we first need to understand the meaning of life, who we are, where we come from, where we are going, and the purpose of our earthly existence. Here is something our teachers have told us:

Our known universe, as well as the universes unknown to us, are made up of an energy that comes from the great fountain of life we call God, or the Creator, or the Great Ultimate, or just universal consciousness. This energy resonates in various ways, at different rhythms or vibrational frequencies, thus forming diverse manifestations of physicality and consciousness. God is unending movement and growth; He could not be unmoving or He would cease to be. As life is change and motion, utter stillness would constitute death. Thus, God chose, and chooses even now, to self-manifest by expanding into multitudinous forms and then reabsorb them into the Whole.

In the beginning, only He existed. As He became aware of His own existence, he wanted to experiment with His experience of Himself and so self-divided into minute particles, giving each the will to do as it pleased. His essence is pure consciousness, which includes the qualities of infinite wisdom, love, compassion, balance, harmony, and joy. And so began creation. Those sparks of consciousness created the various dimensions using the raw material of the Creator, or universal energy. We can say, then, that God manifests by way of His creations and lives through them.

As God's energy materializes, beings arise that are direct emanations of His essence and who therefore bear His essence into different realities and universes. Those entities, having great power and intelligence, are responsible for the creation of worlds and of creatures to serve as vessels for the sparks of divine consciousness that continue to evolve. This physical universe that we humans inhabit, is the densest of all realms and so is where we have come to verify our true nature. For it is exactly this density into which we must submerge ourselves to forget who we are and where we come from.

*As human beings, we are evolving creatures. Having come from the Divine Light, light is all we are and all we knew. In order to understand God's greatness, wisdom, and magnificence, we must isolate ourselves and experience what **Is Not**. We have to enter an illusory dualistic world where everything has an opposite: light* *and darkness, good and evil, pleasure and pain, joy and suffering. "Go out from Paradise, and eat from the tree of knowledge, both good and evil."*

*While we were a part of the Absolute, we could not truly appreciate our magnificence, for we'd never experienced anything to compare it to. Though only He truly existed, in order to truly know Himself, God needed to invent an opposite of some sort: separateness, egotism, cruelty, and fear. So we live these experiences, along with their inharmonious effects, in order to realize what we truly are: love, faith and harmony. By experiencing the illusion and its hollow results, we gradually come to understand what **Is** through its juxtaposition to what **Is Not**.*

What was our purpose for descending into the densest recesses of creation? Visiting other dimensions stimulates our creativity. As emissaries of God's creation, we wish to experience every kind of situation, even the most difficult. Our desire to fully understand our true nature and that of the Infinite has led us to limit ourselves so that later we can truly enjoy unlimitedness. Once we sink into this plane and forget who we truly are, we experience loneliness, abandonment, and overwhelming fear. It is fear that drives this world and gives birth to an ego that needs to feel superior to others, to be recognized by the world, and to possess material things and a sense of control.

Along the road to recovering our true identity there are many bumps along the way. We human beings often become entangled in trivialities that are usually about supporting the ego, in other words, fear. As long as we fail to understand that we are never alone, that we form part of the Whole, and that we do not require the ego, nor its long list of needs, in order to be happy, we will not be able to access the abundance that is to be had through unified consciousness.

In a message about desires they said:

The biggest sacrifice we must make is to eradicate our earthly desires, which are always driven by fear and which lead us to seek abundance where it cannot be found. Our desires are attempts to alleviate our loneliness, but once we understand that the only possible way to eliminate fear and loneliness is through our connection with the Whole, we will no longer need to satisfy any earthly desire.

Human love is necessary because through it we seek the unity that we have lost in our consciousness; love is reunification with God. Knowing our unity is not the same as feeling it at the core of our being; yet, the more we become aware of it, the more familiar our souls will be with the concept. Little by little, we lose the need for a love arrangement with another human being. When we enter into relationship with the higher self, we will experience true abundance and so will no longer need to find it outside of ourselves, for we will be experiencing the deepest and truest union.

All that comes from the Creator must return to Him. First one must distance oneself from the original Source through a process called involution, and then one returns through the process of evolution. In reality, we are never distant for we are always a part of Him, sustained by His divine will. Separation refers to a state of consciousness in which, after descending into the density of the physical world, we lose awareness of our true essence and origin. Returning to Him means reopening our consciousness to the Divinity that lies at the core of each of us.

God gave individuality and free will to the particles of His consciousness that constitute the essence of each human being, so that we would create worlds and realities to express His essence. We are the means for his manifestation, and He has given us the freedom to experience life however we desire. *Life* refers to the dual process of involution and evolution, from the moment of our individualization until the moment of our reunification with the Whole. Our experiences are His, for He is in all that exists. It is His will that it be this way even for the tiniest of His creatures. Hence the proverb: "A leaf cannot fall from a tree without the will of God."

We are the material manifestation of Pure Consciousness, which is the mind from which all creation emanates. Creation springs from movement, and His will is to express Himself thus. We are the vessels of His creative intelligence; however that may be expressed through the myriad individuated intelligences of creation. Our experiences, and those of the angels, and all creatures at every level of the vibrational scale, nourish Him as he moves and expands through all creative acts everywhere. For example, in the case of those of us who have descended to the physical world, we create each one of our experiences here, first the obstacles, and then the ways we resolve them. This is the grand scheme of life: to prove ourselves worthy of the creative power that has been granted us. This is what the dualistic experience is about; to develop our creativity in a thousand ways until we find our way out of the maze. Although God grants us the freedom to do what we will, in fact, His will is ours, and through His laws all will return to harmony; that is to say, it will return to Him.

We cannot understand infinity with such a finite tool as the rational minds. Comprehending the mysteries of creation is not yet within our grasp. But as our consciousness rises to higher levels, we will have a better understanding of these cosmic truths.

The following is a message from a soul already in the spirit world:

> *The truth is within each individual, but as long as we have not achieved cosmic consciousness, we cannot understand its totality. Once we are disembodied, we understand the concepts with much more clarity, as we are no longer immersed in the density of our physical bodies. We will not reach the Creator's wisdom, however,*

until we have passed through all the stages that lead us back to Him.

Oftentimes we believe there is only one path to God, the one each of us has chosen as our own. Everyone believes they possess the absolute truth while everyone else is wrong. Yet the actual state of human consciousness is a thousand light years away from being able to receive and understand divine truth in its totality—. The different concepts that humans have are but glimpses of what truly is. It is not that some of us are right and others wrong. Rather, some aspects of our beliefs correspond to one aspect of the truth, interpreted by way of our limited awareness.

How can the Creator favor any of his children over the others if He loves us all the same? Why would he reveal Himself to only a select few of the billions of human beings that have lived on our planet? We all have within our being that spark of His consciousness where the absolute truth burns. The point is to manifest that truth. But if, instead of eradicating the ego, which believes it possesses the truth, we become dogmatic, we will be covering the internal light that can only emerge by way of humility and love. The day our posture is that we do not possess the truth but rather are open to receiving it, we will have gone far toward actually finding it.

There are many paths to the Creator, and all lead to Him, even those paths that are mistaken, for it is from mistakes that we learn. But the most certain thing we can know is that any true path must be walked with an attitude of love and humility. Our acts of love and humility demonstrate that we are a manifestation of The Almighty, as is the rest of creation, and that superiority and inferiority do not exist in any of His many realms. There are only different levels of evolution and purpose. We owe our existence to Him and his wish to create.

There are many philosophical concepts that will always escape our comprehension, but if we devote ourselves to His will and live a life of faith and humility, our understanding will clarify. Mankind's eternal problem is his arrogance in believing that he is always right, as well as the desire to manipulate those around him by imposing his own beliefs. These are the reasons behind sectarianism and division. But the time is coming for a new human consciousness in which fractiousness will be replaced by a new universal religion based simply on love.

In order to exist, all physical matter must be animated by a spiritual core. It becomes denser at the beginning of the evolutionary process in order to inhabit the mineral kingdom. As the vibration of minerals occur at a very low frequency, one spiritual core or soul group can animate a great number of minerals, giving them energy and life. It simply has to resonate in unison with the mineral's atoms.

After gaining experience in the mineral kingdom its vibrations become more refined and is now ready to energize the vegetable kingdom, where, what we call life exists and a certain kind of sensitivity is experienced.

When it finishes its experience in the vegetable plane it then integrates into the animal realm. It brings its experiences from the mineral and vegetable world vibrating more and more at a higher rate and animating less and less subjects.

The more elevated is the form of life, the soul group becomes more individuated and the higher its state of consciousness. The human soul requires spiritual elements from the mineral, vegetable, and animal realms in order to adapt to the physical world.

The soul is the receptacle of the spark of divine consciousness, which, in order to experience the three dimensional world enters in a physical body. The divine spark has no emotions, no survival instincts required for self-conservation and adaptation to the physical realm. All of this it takes from the spiritual element of the animal kingdom. Thus the human soul is prepared for the physical world experience.

Thus is creation accomplished in stages, first in mineral form, then in plant form, and finally in animal form, culminating in human life.

Different Levels of Consciousness, or Dimensions

The physical world that we know through our five senses is not the only reality. The universe is made up of energy that vibrates at different frequencies, resulting in various levels of experience just as real as this one. Jesus said, "In my Father's house are many mansions," in reference to these different levels that range from the physical world to the original mind of the Creator. The so-called dead only change realities; they don't go anywhere. The different levels interpenetrate, just as our bodies are present in many overlapping dimensions at the same moment.

> *All that can be, is, and exists here. There are not different places but only different vibrational frequencies. The physical universe that an embodied being perceives is just as infinite as other vibrational realms. That which we call God is all of these levels and everything they contain, not something or someone separate from its creation. It is said that the physical universe is infinite because it is not contained within a measurable space. This is the physical manifestation of the Creator's limitlessness. When one is absorbed, the other expands endlessly, and this we call infinity.*

When referring to the different dimensions of consciousness, we're speaking of the different stages one must pass through in developing the qualities of God latent within us. The different dimensions are not to be understood as places but rather as states of consciousness, vibrational planes that come into view as one resonates higher. There are said to be seven vibrational planes, but each has countless sub-levels and vibrational nuances, so the number seven is not to be taken too literally.

The present level, that of human life, is known as the third dimension, wherein we humans forget our true purpose, that of manifesting the divine energy at our core. In this dimension, we feel separated from the rest of creation and so experience fear. This we try to overcome by seeking recognition and social acceptance, by controlling others, and by gathering possessions, all of which are ego-driven attachments to the hollow appeasements of the physical world. In order to transcend the limits of this dimension, we must pass through many varied experiences that help us to see our non-identity with the ego and once more experience unity.

Once we pass through the learning stages that help us eradicate the ego, we no longer need to incarnate into human form. We then pass on to the fourth dimension and are no longer subject to death nor limited by space and time. This is what is meant by "the resurrection." Once we have learned to act from love and to accept our oneness with all of creation, we open to the consciousness of the fifth dimension in which wisdom or knowledge of the cosmic laws and understanding of the plan of creation is obtained.

We then reach the consciousness of the sixth dimension in which the gift of creativity attains its plenitude in total harmony with the cosmic order. This dimension ends in a movement towards the understanding and complete acceptance of the fact that we have never been separate from anything, towards union with the All.

The seventh dimension has been defined as the fusion with the Whole and is impossible to describe, we will just call it God.

The meaning of this long evolutionary process is the expansion of universal consciousness, to open to one's own light, to awaken to who we really are.

The Seven Bodies

The human being is made up of seven bodies, each composed of distinct vibrational frequencies that interpenetrate and interact. The physical body is the only one accessible to the five senses, but there are others, each a different aspect of existence and awareness. The seven bodies can be thought of as energy layers. Everything obeys thought, and the various bodies are emanations of active thought. Each belongs to and acts within a different dimension; thus, we are multidimensional beings, despite our fascination with the physical plane.

The spirit, or pure consciousness, unfolds by becoming more dense in various ways, resulting in form on seven different levels. First we will speak of the major triad of the spiritual body, the causal body, and the higher mental body. The spiritual body is the divine spark; the causal body is the energetic layer in which the experiences during the whole process of manifestation and evolution are recorded; the higher mental body is where thoughts originating from spirit are processed. Then there are four less refined bodies, beginning with the lower mental body, which receives egocentric thoughts. Next is the astral, or emotional, body where the emotions necessary to three-dimensional living are generated. There is also a double ethereal body, which receives the universal energy that gives life to the seventh body, the physical body.

Our various bodies are actually layers of energy with different vibrational frequencies. The densest is the physical body, which basically runs on electricity. It is composed of physical matter, which is energy resonating at a very low frequency. But the physical body is also animated by its ethereal counterpart, the double ethereal body, which is indispensable for cohesion of the body's atoms. This double ethereal element is present in any object formed from physical matter. As its name indicates, this body is composed of universal energy, and its function is to focus that energy into each of the physical body's atoms. The result is an exact replica of the human body. At the moment of death, the ethereal double, also called the bioplasmic body, separates from the physical body and gradually disintegrates. These two bodies, which in effect are one, are the mortal part of the human being.

The astral, or emotional, body is the second densest. This is where all emotions, desires, passions and sensations are stored. It is the energetic template from which the physical body is generated. The emotional body has the same shape as the physical body but is made of far subtler vibrations and exists on the astral level. It is in this body where diseases generate and then manifest in the physical body. Its life lasts as long as its passage through the third dimension. It is composed of mental waves, and contracts when it is time to create another life form. When a divine spark decides to embark on an experience in the physical world, the astral body contracts and enters the body of the mother-to-be, whose genes shape it accordingly, and a new human is born.

The astral body is very sensitive to the emotions, and its vibrations become more elevated as strong emotional reactions subside. Once the separatist ego dissolves and the need for human incarnation has ended, this body disintegrates. In this sense, the astral body is the vessel that we use to enter and exit the physical world. Once that need is transcended, it ceases to be.

The mental body, as mentioned, is a subtle body that functions in two ways. Its lower aspect serves to process thoughts rising from our lower selves, while its higher aspect processes thoughts originating in the spiritual realm. This subtle body serves as the link between the two. This is where thoughts, beliefs and knowledge originate, and where all thoughts, negative and positive, are stored. The latter are those ideas that help us grow and develop. The influence of the mental body over the three lower bodies is decisive. The three lower bodies come into balance and perfection when the lower mental body is refined through meditation, self-observation and the transmutation of thoughts. As long as our attention is focused solely on worldly matters and desires, though, we are unable to access the thoughts coming from spirit.

It is in the lower mental body that judgments, attitudes, and other rigid structures in our way of thinking, establish themselves. Here, egoic thoughts created by feelings of separation and vulnerability are formed. The more rigid our mental body becomes, the more difficult it is for us to flow with life, to learn new ways of living, and to acquire new ideas that are necessary to move forward in our evolutionary development. The mental body is the instrument used by spirit to refine the denser lower bodies. It is the meeting point between the material and the spiritual, as active thought is where the quality of matter originates. Thus, our thoughts weigh either for or against cosmic balance and are responsible for human actions and the reactions they evoke, both cause and effect. If the mind's thoughts are more refined, the material of the lower bodies also become more refined. The mental body does not eventually disappear like the astral. It simply accelerates its vibration until it receives only the loving thoughts coming from the Higher self. The lower aspect of the mental body then dissolves into light.

Actions are conscious and come from the mental body, whereas reactions or those acts we call instinctive, come from the emotional body. In today's world, we continue for the most part to react to stimuli from the emotional body. The emotional and lower mental bodies serve us by making it possible for us to experience duality, but their content can be either positive or negative.

Less dense still is the causal body, which records everything we experience during our lengthy evolutionary process. As the word *causal* indicates, this body is at cause. From it comes the personality, meaning the qualities, tendencies, passions, and aversions acquired by human beings along the path to perfection. It is also where karma is inscribed. The causal body is where reside our core characteristics, with which, and against which, we must work in order to advance along the path of evolution.

Once the lower bodies have been purified, the mental and causal bodies continue their ascent toward the higher planes, eventually turning into light.

Finally we come to the spiritual body, which is the highest body and the one that generates the other six. In order to discover the spiritual body, we must work on accelerating the vibrations of the other bodies. This may be a very involved process, but it is exactly this discovery that we all live for. The spiritual body is the seat of intuition, and the more open we are to spirit, the more precise is our intuition. Because most of us are preoccupied with thoughts coming from the ego, our intuition usually goes unheeded.

The physical body, of course, manifests in the three-dimensional matrix. This is the plane where thought appears to us as solid matter.

When we manifest in the physical world, our attention and thoughts become fixed here, and we can become oblivious to our other realities and other bodies. Then, when we leave the three-dimensional world through the process of physical death, our thoughts may be trapped in this world, where they continue to manifest. Ideally, the vibrational level of our thoughts is sufficiently elevated at the moment of death to manifest at a higher plane of consciousness. This process of acceleration, or transmutation, of the vibrations of the emotional, mental and causal bodies continues until all turns into light and merges with the Creator.

From each of these bodies an aura emanates, which is the electromagnetic field enfolding and surrounding every living being.

Death and the Astral Plane

During the first phase of what we call death, the higher bodies separate from the two perishable bodies, and we can see the spent physical body as though it belongs to someone else.

Meanwhile, we find ourselves in another body seemingly as solid and real as the physical. This occurs when one shifts his or her manifestation to the astral plane. They are still enveloped in a form, or energy mold, the same one that produced the physical body.

The astral plane is the spiritual world which belongs to the third dimension, and it consists of three principal levels, each divided into various spheres according to their vibrational frequency. It is on these various levels of the astral that souls in transit are found, waiting to either reincarnate or continue evolving until they can access the next plane, the fourth dimension.

In the lower astral are disembodied beings with sluggish vibrations due to their strong attachment to the earthly plane. Those who find themselves here, depending on their state of consciousness, are in what is considered to be "purgatory" or "hell". Such a situation, though, is both voluntary and temporary.

Next is the middle astral, which is more refined. At this stage in human evolution, most of those who pass through death find themselves here. The higher reaches of the astral are where more evolved souls are to be found. From the higher astral, one may either pass to the fourth dimension or choose to return to the earthly plane in to help others.

Upon arriving at any level of the astral plane, the soul may feel disoriented due to the novelty of the situation. However, if we surrender to God, either just before or after the moment of death, and asks for aid—which is very common—a light immediately appears. In cases where the self is greatly attached to what it has left behind, it is temporarily unable to travel to the plane where it belongs, and it will find itself surrounded by darkness. It is at these moments that the assistance of those of us still on earth can be of great help. We intervene with prayer, or by speaking to them directly, and we can be heard because the vibration of the recently disembodied still has an affinity to that of the physical plane.

While on earth, we all attribute value to what in fact has none, and generally allow ourselves to be carried away by our impulses and desires. When we reach "the other side," we realize that all we valued is actually of no use.

So-Called Death is Really Resurrection

I lived attached to everything I found beautiful, be it women, cars, works of art, houses, whatever my money could buy. Nothing else had value except what I desired, and any way I could get them was fine.

I died suddenly, at a time when I was stealing whatever I fancied and doing so without guilt. I didn't consider it a bad thing because I saw the world as a jungle where it was every man for himself. My conscience was asleep and overwritten by my desires. Every time I was able to acquire something I'd yearned for, I felt great joy. But, oh, how brief that pleasure was, like a shooting star. So I would immediately turn all my attention and energies to some new interest. Then I arrived at this place. I was expecting nothing. For me, death meant nothingness, so I was very surprised to find myself alive in an unfamiliar place.

I don't know how long I've been here, but I can tell you that I experienced anger and despair at having lost all that once belonged to me. I saw no sense in it, and I could find no solace. At last, I began to think about the life I had led. Once you don't have a physical body, it is easier to understand more of what life is about. I realized that my life had been led by my desire to possess and control everything around me. I saw that this wasn't right. How did I come to this conclusion? By analyzing my feelings. I realized that my misbehavior had never given me peace and harmony; there was always a feeling of unease and dissatisfaction. Then I recalled all the times I had helped someone, or sympathized with someone, and how I'd I felt afterwards. That feeling did fill me with peace and satisfaction.

How can one be so blind during one's time on earth and not see this? We spend our lives struggling to obtain material things, then at the time of our death, these things are completely useless. We do this instead of making choices that will lead us to true and lasting happiness.

I now find myself in a place that is less dark, but without quite knowing what to do. I hear voices calling me and telling me to go toward the light, but I don't see it. Instead I was brought to you. Can you tell me what to do?

The above request came to us from a disembodied soul we'd had no previous contact with. As we always do in these situations, we explained his situation to him and told him how to reach the light. At the end, he said to us:

I feel drawn by a light that I cannot describe. It looks like a whirlwind of colors opening into a light of incredible brightness, yet the light isn't blinding. As I approach closer, it becomes greater and brighter. How could I have so stubbornly denied the existence of God? This is Heaven. I see people calling to me. I am leaving. ... Thank you ... I now understand what life is. And so-called death is really resurrection.

Here is a message that came to us regarding egocentrism:

An egocentric individual is never happy. In fact, people of this sort are often quite neurotic. This is due to the fact that, by being egocentric, they drift away from their true self, their essence, by focusing solely on their personality. It is this separatist attitude that believes it will find happiness in flattery, popularity, and superiority over others. This will actually bring nothing but frustration, for it will not fill the existential void within any who consciously separate from the great Whole.

When we seek to fill this void with material objects, sensory pleasures, money, fame, or power, we find that every desire fulfilled is immediately followed by yet another. And, honestly, each fulfillment feels hollow because it is so ephemeral. Money does not bring happiness, and fame and power only isolate us more from our fellow human beings.

This self-defeating attitude is very painful because we are acting completely at odds with what we are and what we unconsciously long for, namely unity with all that exists. The feelings of separateness and superiority merely accentuate the soul's desolation at having lost the unity awareness.

The only thing that brings true happiness is unconditional love because we were made from this. When we act with unconditional love, we are acting in accordance with what we truly are.

Speaking to "La Cabrita"

This case is special to us because it came with verifiable evidence. A woman named Teresina who attended one of our meditation groups astonished us with her special faculties. As a medium and clairvoyant, not only could she see other planes of reality, but she was able to act as an intermediary, allowing other beings to speak using her voice.

During one of our group meditation sessions, Eduardo, a departed soul whom we already knew, communicated with us through Teresina's voice. Because of the very rigid and strict life Eduardo had led, we'd never considered that he might need our help, but through Teresina, Eduard criticized us about the lack of help he had received from us. We admitted we had not realized he required it, despite the countless messages he had sent us.

Eduardo, we learned, was unable to leave the lower astral plane because of his guilt and fear of the punishment he thought would surely come. Eduardo had very rigid religious beliefs that hindered rather than aided his spiritual progress. We prayed, counseled him, and managed to convince him to proceed to the light. Before leaving, Eduardo said:

Thank you for helping me so much. Continue to help those who are trapped. There are millions and millions like me. I am with Julio. You can help him by telling his daughter, 'La Cabrita,' that he is all right. This will bring him peace.

We were then given a telephone number and told to ask for Elena.

While this last conversation was taking place, our clairvoyant, Teresina, clearly saw the aforementioned man, Julio, drowning in the sea. We felt unsettled by this information and unsure of what to do with it. We decided to call the number and ask for Elena. After a moment, she came to the phone. We briefly explained why we were calling, and Elena immediately broke down in tears, saying that her father had in fact drowned eighteen years before.

A few days later, we met with Elena to meditate and send light to her father. She told us that since his death she had not stopped thinking of him and wondering where he was, constantly calling for him and torturing herself with thoughts of what he must have suffered at his death. She was shocked to learn that he had referred to her by her nickname "La Cabrita." This was a term of affection that Elena's own children had given her, not her father. This convinced her of the veracity of what we'd told her and that her father had been with her the entire time. This was a huge release for both of them, and Julio was able to rise to the plane where he belonged, and Elena felt peace knowing that her father was well and happy.

From these examples, we can see how intense mourning for someone can actually keep our loved ones stuck in a place neither here nor there. The suffering of loved ones left behind can disturb the departed to the point where they cannot elevate themselves from limbo. It may sound very easy to convince such wandering souls to let go of their earthly interests, so one may question why it is so difficult to convince those with whom we have direct communication. This is due to the clarity with which we see matters of the spirit once we shed the physical body. It's true, as well, that once we go into the light, our level of understanding is clarified, affording us astonishing objectivity.

2

Detachment

~

When we have done all the work we
were sent to Earth to do,
We are allowed to shed our body,
which imprisons our soul
Like a cocoon encloses the future butterfly.
And when the time is right, we can let go of it
And we will be free of pain, free of fears and worries—
Free as a very beautiful butterfly, returning home to
God.
~Elisabeth Kubler-Ross

J ust as Elisabeth Kubler-Ross has defined the stages of dying that precede death, there are also stages that come after the moment of death. One does not attain the wisdom of "the beyond" by simply having left the body. A long period of adjustment to this new condition will be necessary. After separation of the two perishable bodies, one finds oneself in the same basic state of consciousness and evolution as just before death. The individual retains his or her desires and beliefs, interests and prejudices, as well as mistaken ideas and religious distortions.

Generally, the being who has just died needs a certain amount of time to completely detach from his or her body, so it's very common for them to remain close to the body for a while. Most civilizations believe that the spiritual body completely separates from the physical body in three days. Based on this belief, Tibetans allow for a lapse of time before cremating the body. However, not all separations occur in the same way. Some individuals need less time, and others may take longer, depending on the circumstances of death or their level of evolution.

In many cases, beings detach very quickly from the physical body and quickly experience the inexpressible joy of merging with the light. In other cases, however, they remain strongly attached to the physical body and to their former lives, clinging to them. This traps them in the limbo of the lower astral plane, which is neither the material world nor the world of spirit. Some are not even aware they have died, instead feeling despair at their sudden inability to be seen and heard. Others realize they have passed away but, for any number of reasons, refuse to move on. These reasons can range from absolute denial of their own spiritual essence, which situation is referred to as *hell*; or to a sense of guilt, or the fear of punishment, or simple defiance at what has happened, which condition is referred to as *purgatory*. There are many reasons why a soul might refuse to follow the call to the light; but pride seems always to be the motivating force behind such reasons. In death, just as in life, we are the architects of our own destiny.

The simplest way to help these stymied souls is by praying that they will detach themselves from the relatively low vibrations of the earthly plane. They can also be helped by explanations, through a medium, that they no longer belong in the physical world and that they need to seek the light.

In some cases, what prevents them from rising to the higher spheres is an unfocused attachment to what they have left behind, be it material possessions, power, or special relationships.

The following is what the masters have to say in regard to the separation of those who experienced worldly power and fame:

Power and fame are two of the greatest obstacles to overcome because those who have enjoyed them only to die at the pinnacle of their domination, believe they have lost everything, and they despair at their inability to continue commanding and manipulating others.

When such individuals arrive in the astral wrapped in despair at having lost their power, they listen to no one. Time must pass. Gradually, they are forgotten on earth and supplanted by another powerbroker. Only then do such souls come out of their denial, for now they see what happens to power and fame once we die. Usually, the main issue in these cases is that such beings do not believe in the existence of life after death. Though they may acknowledge that they are still alive, the darkness in which they find themselves seems to reaffirm the belief that death is darkness and nothingness.

How many beings find themselves in these conditions? A great many, and they need the prayers of those still on earth, as prayer energy can help free them from the pull of earthly vibrations.

Even after a soul's liberation from the lower astral plane and its arrival in the spiritual realm, it can continue to be influenced by its memories of earthly glory.

Returning to the physical world after having experienced fame is not easy; one must first experience being a "nobody." This takes a great deal of courage, which is not acquired quickly, especially when worldly fame continues, or even increases, after death. Take, for instance, a famous musician whose music continues to be heard after his death. The vibration of humanity's admiration continues to reach that musician and feed his ego, despite his removal to the world of spirit and his having understood certain things. He may continue to have an appetite for success. This can be a strong feeling and not at all easy to overcome. Nonetheless, the desire to move forward is there as well, and may prove stronger than the desire for more human glory.

Sometimes a soul such as this decides to return to earth in order to learn humility. He or she needs to experience extremely precarious conditions, maybe reincarnating as someone with very limited intelligence or financial resources, so that he or she can never truly flourish. This occurs when the call of the Supreme Being is stronger than the soul's memories of success.

People who spend their lives controlling those around them tend to suffer greatly after death, as they can no longer continue dominating others. The problem with many powerful men is that they continue to try to impose their will from the astral plane, which keeps them from ascending.

I Can't Leave Him Here!

The young man on the phone is nervous and quiet. Rolando has difficulty explaining his problem yet dodges our questions and constantly defends himself. But because we can sense his deep sadness, Carmen and I go to see him. We're surprised to find this young man the owner of an enormous mansion that houses impeccably preserved antique European furniture, as well as many valuable paintings and objects of silver. "It's my inheritance from my uncle," explains Rolando. After several long pauses, he tells us he feels his uncle's presence in the house. Since his uncle's death several years before, Rolando has been unable to escape a deep depression, due first to his uncle's absence and secondly to his inability to establish a happy life. Despite the young man's stammering and hesitancy, we learn that the authoritarian uncle, Francisco, was extremely possessive toward his young nephew.

"I'm not sure if the presence here is your uncle," said Carmen. "It could be another entity, and I don't like to begin this kind of communication with assumptions. Let's meditate, asking for protection and establishing the intention of helping whoever is here."

In the midst of our meditation, we began receiving the following message:

Thank God I can finally express myself! It's me, Francisco! For a long time I've wanted to communicate with my dearest Rolando and have been unable to do so. I've wanted to tell you that I've been by your side to guide you through this harsh physical world. Ever since I left you, I've been unable to see anything beyond this house and you, my beloved. I know only that I want to be near you, but you do not hear me, and that drives me to despair.

We answered by explaining to the departed uncle that he should no longer be concerned with the world, that he is meant to be enjoying a very rewarding life on some other plane. This led to an objection:

I can't leave him here! He doesn't know how to deal with the jungle of humanity. He is much too sensitive and delicate to be left alone. Don't ask me to leave him. It pains me too much.

"It's now his time to live independently from you. He must learn to struggle alone in order to become stronger. You, on the other hand, must continue evolving by seeking the light of God that's always available to those who ask for it. God is infinite love and mercy, and He is waiting for you to return to Him, for you to leave that place and look for the light. It will be there for you."

I don't know who you are, but you're saying very beautiful things. True, I have always believed in God, but not in the way I was taught. I was told there would be a hell for sinners, and a purgatory to experience before getting to heaven. It isn't so. Here there is nothing but cold and darkness. The only sight that reaches me here is that of the one I left behind and whom I still love dearly.

We focused on sending Francisco loving energy.

I don't know what you're sending me, but I feel a sense of warmth and wellbeing. It would be great if I could always feel this way.

We said, "You will feel all of that and much more. You see only darkness now because your thoughts are keeping you in the dark. Your desire to protect your loved one is preventing you from seeing the light."

I'm asking from the bottom of my heart. Now I see a glimpse of light. It's very comforting in this cold, dank dungeon. It's getting brighter and brighter. But what about Rolando? Do I have to desert him?

We asked Rolando to mentally urge his uncle to follow the light, where he would find peace and happiness. Finally, Francisco responded to him directly:

Okay, dear boy. If you ask for it, so it will be. I will go toward that light I can't describe. It's surrounding me. I feel an indescribable sense of joy. How could I not have seen it for so long? I understand now what hell is, and what they call purgatory. It's our own blindness that prevents us from seeing past our desires. I see now that all I ever wanted was for things to go my way. I tried to impose my will on those around me. You gave me so much love and satisfaction, Rolando, and I was always so cruel and selfish toward you. My love was possessive and dictatorial. Forgive me. I think this light illuminates the truth. I'm starting to see things with amazing clarity.

I will go into this light that I cannot resist. I know that I will be able to help you better from there.

I Couldn't Get Over Having Lost Power and Control

A soul once came to us who had gone through a similar problem of power and control. This is what he shared with us:

I suffered greatly after my death. Suddenly I found myself in a cold, dark place. I wanted to continue controlling and enjoying everything as I had in life. During my final days on earth, my physical suffering was such that I did wish for death, but after leaving behind everything I'd ever loved, I felt even worse.

The grief of my wife, who had lived only for me, kept me stuck here for a long time. Worse, I couldn't get over having lost the control and the power I'd once held over those around me.

I don't know how long, in earthly time, this hell lasted, but I lost my way due to pride and my desire for power and control. It was very painful for me to watch all the legal disputes over my estate, and I promised myself I would never again succumb to the desire to possess. It was a great lesson in detachment. Now I will have to experience a lifetime of deprivation in order to master detachment and humility.

I do not yet have the strength to take on such a life, but I know it will come in due course. All I can tell you is that now that I have transcended attachment to power and control. I am happy, and I don't want to go through that again.

I Need my Daughter's Forgiveness to be Able to Find Rest

There are cases in which feelings of guilt keep a soul in the lower astral plane. In the following case, the soul in question was suffering remorse because he had been very dictatorial with his family and caused them great unhappiness. After physical death, he'd spent many years in his guilt-infused hell. Finally, he approached Carmen asking her to tell his daughter how much he regretted having behaved the way he had, and that he needed her forgiveness in order to be able to find rest.

We agreed to speak with his daughter, after which we received the following message:

> *My daughter's forgiveness was the greatest gift you could have given me. Of course, she may have spoken well of me because that's her way. She would never speak badly of her family. But I made her, and my sweet wife, suffer by imposing my will on them. In earthly time, I don't know how long I've been here with this guilt that overpowered me while reviewing my life. I had been loving toward my family, but always on my own terms, and I had never cared what they might want or think. I believe you're telling me that we all make mistakes, and this is why we come to physical life; by experiencing darkness we learn to understand the light. I am now ready to go toward this light you have told me about. I will call for it now and so leave this place forever behind.*

Time doesn't exist on the other side of the veil, but the intensity of our thoughts and feeling can create an illusion of time. The more we obsess over thoughts of guilt, revenge, attachment, or hate, the longer it will seem before our soul finds peace and crosses over to the light.

Guilt Is Nothing More Than Pride

In effect, guilt is an unwillingness to accept our imperfection. It's one thing to become aware of our mistakes and learn from them, so as not to repeat them. It's a very different matter to become mired in guilt as a result of our arrogance in not accepting that we are imperfect. The need to be forgiven is based on our desire to be accepted by those we've hurt, and this is also a form of pride.

The following is a case in point, told by soul who had realized this important lesson:

> *I've spoken to you before. You did me the favor of passing along a message to my children, who didn't believe it. But this doesn't matter anymore because I've come to understand many things since then. Desiring forgiveness from those who suffered because of our mistakes is nothing more than pride. We can't stand our own imperfection, or being seen as imperfect by others. By humbling ourselves to ask for forgiveness, we demonstrate our desire for the acceptance of those we've offended. I understand that now, and it's no longer guilt that plagues me but personal remorse at having acted so superficially and selfishly.*

Having freed himself from guilt, this soul was able to find the light.

Some people, because of their rigid religious beliefs, do not open themselves to new concepts for fear of breaking with established norms. Our guides say the following in reference to this:

> *Each individual is responsible for his own spiritual evolution, and there is nothing we can do about it. There are many who fear facing themselves honestly and taking responsibility for their own acts. This is why people hide behind established beliefs directed by others, rather than*

thinking for themselves and embarking on a personal quest for light and truth, with no institutions to back them up.

But human consciousness must rise from the infantile state in which it has lingered for so long. Awareness develops as a result of a personal search for the light by an adult deciding and acting for him- or herself, not depending on dogmas and rules established by those who pretend to have a monopoly on divine revelation.

Divine revelation is nothing more than accessing one's own light. As we open ourselves to divine wisdom, which is part of our own essence, it will manifest. This is the heritage of all human beings, not just a few "chosen ones." If we settle for the concepts given to us, neither questioning them nor trying to get to the bottom of them, we will be unable to evolve our consciousness. We will remain in an infantile state, accepting without question what has been told to us.

Our obsession to compel others to believe and think as we do, is nothing more than the ego. Fanaticism is, in fact, a mixture of, first, the fear of facing ourselves and taking responsibility for our own acts, and secondly the desire to control and manipulate others. It's also the fear of adopting new patterns of behavior and thought. Those who become religious or ideological zealots are those who lack the courage to change.

When we leave the physical body behind and reach the world of spirit, there is no longer a place for fanaticism. There we see our own acts with an objective clarity that precludes self-justification. The argument that we were just going along with this rule or that dogma, no longer works. There is only our own judgment of what we did, either acting with love or without it. We have run out of religious excuses and pretexts of having acted according to what we'd been taught. If it was done without love, that's just the truth of it.

When we find ourselves facing judgment concerning the life we have lived, it is usually our misguided acts and omissions that bother us most. But our remorse provides the greatest lesson because it etches our errors on our causal body and so keeps us from repeating those behaviors in future experiences.

A great deal of pain comes from having had opportunities to open ourselves to deep knowledge, yet choosing to remain closed. These missed opportunities are the result of fear. It is usually easier to stay within the bounds of conventional wisdom than to delve into profoundly challenging teachings. The result is regret for those who choose to remain at the superficial level rather than accept the challenge to evolve.

But for all these mistaken attitudes, there is an alternative, that of divine love and mercy that does not judge or punish, but only understands. This light, filled with love, peace, beauty, and harmony, envelops us as soon as we accept it and move toward it. Our Creator is always here, ready and willing to fill us once more with the love our egocentrism has drained away. All we need do is ask for it.

I Don't Know if I Can Face Judgment

This is the case of a deceased priest who, overwhelmed by guilt and afraid of judgment, was unable to see the light. He manifested during one of our prayer group meetings.

I feel very disoriented. I don't know if I deserve punishment which I didn't even believe in, or if I should open myself to a truth I didn't dare accept when I was alive.

We encouraged this soul to seek the light, where he would find peace and divine mercy.

You tell me to call for the light, but it will surely contain the judgment I fear for not having abided by the rules I avowed when becoming a priest. I was a rebel and preached against the dogmas and dictates of the ecclesiastical authorities. I did this for no real reason— just arrogance and hoping to find acceptance from the Christians who were not satisfied with the teaching of the traditional church. I didn't have the courage to set aside my position as a priest and seek the truth with sincerity and devotion. I remained in between, out of fear. Help is being offered to me here, but I don't dare accept it. I don't know if it's a trap that will lead me to hell.

"You think that way because of your mistaken ideas about heaven and hell. Only God's love exists. Purgatory and hell are voluntarily chosen mental states," we said while sending him rose-colored light, which is the energy of love that helps one ascend and see things with clarity."

I feel the love you're sending me, but I don't know if I can face judgment. I'm terrified at the idea of being accused of all the bad things I've done.

"God does not punish. His love and mercy are infinite. Look for the light; it is there. Your new life awaits you, one filled with peace and happiness. Punishment does not exist. Your feelings of guilt are what keep you from seeing it."

Then where are good and evil, if God forgives all?

"Evil does not exist," we explained. "If we understand that God is both all that is and absolutely good, then we know that no opposing force can exist. There is only light. Shadow is just the absence of light; it does not in itself exist. Acts we call evil are just the misguided bungling of human beings suffering from ignorance. The Creator does not punish this but provides opportunities and conditions whereby we learn which road should be taken."

Why then was I taught all those concepts that you say are wrong? It's unbelievable that people continue to be taught erroneous information that causes so much suffering.

We continued to pray and send him light, hoping to convince him.

I think I'm beginning to understand, but you must tell those who haven't yet died that this passage will be difficult if they enter it with guilt and fear of punishment.

Then we heard:

> *I'm going toward the light now. I feel an enormous sense of wellbeing and absolutely no judgment. I perceive only love, love, love. How could I have been so blind? Why didn't I have the courage to go beyond my worries? But The Almighty is infinitely good. He is love, and I think he will forgive my weaknesses. ... You have given me love and confidence. Goodbye, and thank you for your help.*

Guilt is the result of our desire to be perfect and our unwillingness to accept that we all make mistakes. If we could realize that our mistakes are born from a simple lack of consciousness, guilt would not exist. Only the humility to accept our dark side, and the understanding that the darkness will become light once, our consciousness is open to it.

The following is a beautiful message received from our masters:

> *It's not a good idea to be very demanding of ourselves; we must practice tolerance even with ourselves. Once again, we arrive at the concept of balance. This does not mean that we should indulge our faults, nor should we hate them. We need to become aware of them and understand that they are the result of a lack of awareness, and of self-centeredness. When we confront our failings, they gradually lose their power. If we hate them, we're only nurturing them. Why?*
>
> *Hate and rejection are negative energies that become mixed with the very faults we hate, strengthening and nurturing them. If, on the other hand, we are tolerant*

toward them, accepting that we are not yet perfect, our humility generates a positive force that helps eliminate our defects. This is why meditation is a powerful tool in spiritual development. It enables us to see our defects without negativity, thus neutralizing them.

Our desire for perfection is innate because it signifies our desire to return to our true essence, which is perfection. When we return to God, we return to our origin after having undergone multiple experiences that have brought glory to the Creator. If we act negatively, it's because we have lost our way along the journey of creative experimentation. But we can always find it again.

I Thought I Had Bought Salvation

Some departed souls, still bound by human pride, refuse to accept that what they find is not in accordance with their expectations. So they remain in a state of defiance, making evolution temporarily impossible. Ironically, many individuals who believe themselves to be spiritually advanced, are disappointed to find they are not received with honors by the entire celestial court. It can be difficult to help these beings because they won't listen to anything that does not confirm their existing beliefs.

Although Pedro had been bound by strong religious beliefs, his had been a life of arrogance and selfishness. At death, he did not find what he'd expected at death, causing a great deal of despair and angry defiance. Our guides asked us to help Pedro. They told us they had been unsuccessful in all their attempts. His skepticism stemmed from his belief that he knew everything, and that anything that differed from his way of thinking had to be wrong. Pedro thought he'd purchased salvation through donations he had made to the Church. The problem here was not religious beliefs. Where there is no pride, beliefs can be easily modified. It was Pedro's pride that prevented him from accepting that he'd been mistaken; that salvation cannot be bought but must be discovered through love.

We focused on sending Pedro light and love, hoping he would leave his self-chosen confinement. We explained that punishment does not exist, that hell and purgatory are merely mental states. To which he replied:

I have not seen hell because that isn't where I'm supposed to be. But I know it exists because a God who does not punish would not be a just God. I am locked up here in my house because my case has yet to be processed. I always followed the Church's precepts, and I gave money to help spread its doctrines. If I committed any sins, I always confessed them, and that is enough to obtain forgiveness. Now I wait for my angel to come and take me before God.

We tried convincing this confused soul that the only path to God is one of love, plus the humility to accept things as they really are, but we were unsuccessful. Our guides urged us to continue sending him light, as this might help convince him of the error of his belief that he had already earned his salvation. But his pride did not allow him to accept anything he had not previously accepted as true.

We continued to pray for several days, sending Pedro loving energy, praying and insisting that he go toward the light. Finally, one day he reported attaining more clarity:

A wave of warmth, which you have called love, is reaching me. I don't understand anything here since nothing is as I believed it would be. You say it's arrogant to not accept what I'm experiencing, but what is the humility you speak of? If I knew that what you're saying is true, I would go, but I've had a lot of time to reflect, and I have come to realize all the harm I've caused. My life was governed by rancor and envy, and I destroyed everything that crossed my path. This weighs terribly on me now, and I don't think I deserve any glory at all. I was blinded by my pride in demanding that things be as I saw fit, but I now realize this is not the way, and I'm afraid. Yes, I'm afraid of the punishment that I know I deserve.

"Punishment does not exist," we replied. "God is love and therefore does not punish, but rather waits with infinite patience for us to become aware of the only true path that exists. To be humble is to know that no one is superior to anyone else, that we are all different manifestations of the same essence, and that each of us has a different function and role to play in the Creator's infinitely wise plan. Once we come to an understanding of this, there is no longer a wish to stand out, or to control others. To be humble means to be aware that everything that happens to us contains a lesson, which is why complete acceptance of our circumstances leads to perfect humility."

For sure, what I'm experiencing now is hell. There must be some kind of mercy for suffering souls. I will listen to the voices I'm hearing that are trying to help me.

It was a beautiful moment when Pedro finally saw the light and allowed himself to be carried away by the beings who had tried so patiently for so long to help him.

Dialogue with a "Demon"

There are some spirits who do not want to believe in powers superior to themselves and so reject their own light by denying the existence of the Source of Life from which they came. These are very unfortunate souls because they can find no solace, and their distress knows no bounds. As we said before, the lower astral plane consists of several layers. These dark beings reside at the level considered to be hell, where anguish and darkness reign supreme. Angels and guides from higher realms descend to these pitiful haunts to help their inhabitants find the light that their arrogance has led them to reject. It's always possible to abandon this dismal plane, as being there is voluntary. The Creator welcomes all creatures to his bosom, without exception. Even Saint Peter, in one of his epistles speaks of Christ after his death: "He went and preached to the spirits in prison because they formerly did not obey" (I Peter 3:19). Were there no salvation, preaching to them would make no sense.

One day we received an anguished phone call from a woman we knew. She and her husband had a teenage son, and the family was close. After a long search, they had found a home that they loved: modern and cozy with a small garden filled with sunshine. They were excited to move in, but the excitement was short-lived. Their son, Daniel, usually enthusiastic about life, had become anxious and ill-tempered. His long silences gave way to inexplicable violent outbursts that eventually began to affect the couple's relationship. The harmony in the family, once their greatest source of satisfaction, had been replaced by its opposite. In a moment of anguish, young Daniel disclosed that he felt as though he were being followed by someone, a presence attached to his body. He would feel the gasping breath of this being next to his face while he wrote. One night he went into his parent's room, terrified. A formless being, a sort of decomposing cadaver, said Daniel, had appeared next to him. His parents tried to calm him down, saying: "It was a nightmare. It's just nerves." But the boy insisted, "I saw it standing next to my bed!"

As the days passed, things grew worse. There were odd incidents that frightened them, preventing the young family from living in peace in their new home. Huge arguments erupted over trivial matters. The husband's job, always successful before, was now mired in difficulties.

We agreed to visit and see if we could help. From the moment we walked in, we knew something was wrong. The atmosphere was heavy. Everything indicated the presence of a disembodied entity. We carried out the usual rituals to help souls in darkness, after which we received the following message:

I'll leave when I damn well please, not when you want me to, you bitches.

From the aggressive and profane manner of his speech, we knew what kind of spirit we were dealing with. We asked the reason for his remaining in this place.

I followed a friend of the first owner to this house. You would call him a degenerate. I devoted myself to corrupting him as much as I could. Now I intend to lead the young man of this family astray, as well. I lost my body many generations ago and was once desperate at being unable to manifest myself in the world. Now I amuse myself by creating as much chaos as I can for the embodied.

"What do you get out of being where you no longer belong?" we asked. "As you can see, you can no longer manifest yourself on this plane. A much more interesting and pleasant life awaits you, if you simply call for the light."

That's some fantasy people tell themselves. It doesn't exist. You're very naïve to believe what religion teaches. The only thing that exists is what you and I see. There is no light, nor any other life beyond the one I lost, and what little I have now.

"The light exists for those who want to see it. Let's try something. Ask for the light, and let's see what happens," we urged.

That's stupid. I'm not going to ask for any light because I don't believe in it. It goes against my principles. I'm staying here.

"You're wasting your time and an opportunity for a wonderful life, the one God has prepared for all those who wish it. You only need follow the light, which is love, peace and happiness, instead of continuing to cling to what is no longer meant for you."

Ha-ha! You speak to me of God, and I tell you again that you're stupid. God doesn't exist. I am my own God.

Unfortunately, we were unable to convince this soul. He remained shrouded in the darkness he had created by denying God's light and his own. We regretted not being able to help the family, but we did advise them to no longer fall for this being's perverse game. Now that they knew what was going on, they could ignore him and go on with their lives. Such beings are what we call *demons*; souls mired in a hell of their own creation. However, this situation cannot go on forever. The attraction to He who created us is so powerful that someday every soul will forget his or her arrogance and find the way to our final destination, the Source of Light from whence we came. Since God is absolute, there can be nothing that is not in Him, and everything that arises from His essence will sooner or later return to it.

Beings such as the one in this example are obsessed with manifesting themselves again on the physical plane. When they're unable to do so, they spend their time irritating those who can, inducing them to behave inharmoniously. Sometimes they are even able to possess a human being, haunting and driving them to suicide or dementia. Many cases of insanity are caused by such possessions, though psychiatrists usually do not recognize them as such.

A Case of Possession

Demonic possessions do happen. Possession occurs through beings attached to the terrestrial plane who, unable to manifest a body, take over those of others, appropriating their will and absorbing their light.

Clearly, these souls lack spiritual evolution. From what we've seen, such demonic beings live in darkness, feeding on the light of those they harass, preferring those who possess some type of psychic ability, with whom they are able to establish close contact.

I (Carmen) once had the opportunity to witness exactly such a possession, at a moment when I could very well have been a victim myself. When I'd begun to develop my psychic sensibilities through intuitive writing, I started communicating with other planes and came into contact with lower astral beings. Because they vibrate at very near the earthly plane's low frequency, communication with them is very easy. This is why when playing with a Ouija board it's so easy to establish contact. The only requirement for the link to occur is for one of the participants to have somewhat developed psychic abilities.

Back then, there were many demonic beings who tried to possess me, manipulating me in various ways. The method they prefer is to first appeal to one's ego through flattery. They say that you have an important mission, or that they will tell you how to get what you desire, or that they can help you obtain wisdom—basically, anything to feed your sense of personal importance. At the same time, they attempt to take over your will by making constant demands. Later, they use mockery and humiliation to keep you at their mercy. I understood all this from my own personal experience.

Once at a social gathering, I heard someone mention a poor woman who had been ill for some time. She claimed to hear voices giving her orders all day long, and it was driving her crazy. A psychiatric evaluation had determined that the woman wasn't insane. When I heard what she was going through, I knew she was probably experiencing what had recently happened to me, so I asked a friend of hers to take me to see her.

When we arrived, Veronica was wandering around her house in a bathrobe like a ghost. She seemed surprised and displeased to see me. I later learned that the voices had told her not to see me. I had, in fact, ignored her excuses for not being able to receive us, and had gone to see her anyway.

I asked Veronica what the voices had told her. She did not respond, so I began to suggest what I imagined they might have said, to which she nodded in fearful agreement. Veronica seemed overwhelmed by a terrible nervousness, and it became apparent that she was listening to someone.

"Veronica, are they speaking to you now?" I asked.

"Yes, Carmen. They're saying you should leave," she replied fearfully.

"Tell them that they are the ones who are going to leave. Order them to leave you alone. Tell them you have decided to not listen to them anymore."

I tried to explain to her that she was dealing with negative entities from whom she needed to free herself. Having had the same experience, I knew to a certain extent what needed to be done to be rid of them. The first step is to not let oneself be controlled by these beings, which means trying not to listen to them. If they continue, the only way to push them away is through prayer. By raising her vibration through prayer, she could escape their reach.

Veronica listened carefully but was still hesitant. I took a cross I had brought with me and placed it on her and began reciting psalms and prayers—but her fear would not allow it. She lost control and tore off the cross, ordering me to leave her alone.

A few days later, I told my meditation teacher what had happened, and we decided to visit Veronica together. This teacher, who had helped me rid myself of the entities that had tormented me, knew much more than I did about the matter.

From the moment Veronica opened the door to us, her throat emitted a terrible, threatening snarl. She continued to snarl the entire time we were with her. As before, we explained the situation, telling Veronica she could free herself of her scourges by firmly resolving to banish them and by praying. We sprinkled holy water and began praying out loud. Meanwhile, the snarling intensified, and the poor woman, nervous and restless, began walking in and out of the room until she exclaimed in despair:

"Carmen, please leave! I'm tired!"

From our perspective, it was the uncontrollable snarling from the core of her being that was exhausting her.

For several days, we prayed for Veronica and sent her light. We later heard that she had freed herself of the voices. But they had already absorbed so much of her energy and weakened her to such an extent that she died soon thereafter.

The Obsessors

When death comes to beings in a somewhat primitive state of awareness because of some sort of addiction such as alcohol, drugs, tobacco, sex and the like, such individuals do their best to satisfy these vices through incarnate souls with the same bad habits. They haunt the living and induce them to continue their addictions. Here is what was told to us by a soul who experienced this during his time on earth:

During my life on the earthly plane, there was a being who haunted me and induced me to drink and act with a coarseness atypical of me when I was sober.

When I was under the effects of alcohol, a crack would open in my aura through which this being would enter and take possession of my will. I didn't realize in the moment what was happening, and afterwards I couldn't understand how I could have behaved as I did. He gained more and more power over me over time, always following me, making me obsessed with alcohol and sex.

When I went through physical death, I saw him standing before me, mocking me with his laugher. It was his way of exacting revenge, for he would no longer have my body with which to pursue his vices. There are many disincarnate souls who do this, and it's difficult to convince them to follow the light, but, as always, prayers and love can help.

When we're under the influence of a strong addiction, our vibration slows down, thus weakening our energy field. This makes it easier for disembodied beings with a similar vibration to enter and control us. These beings take pleasure in the influence they have over incarnate beings, whose energy they greedily absorb. There are psychics who can help banish these beings by convincing them to go toward the light, but only if the person being haunted agrees to overcome his vices. If the addicted person does not choose rehabilitation, he will continue to attract these dark beings and their negativity.

The following is an example:

Fernando asked for help from Carmen because everything in his life was going wrong, both financially and emotionally. The session began promptly with these sentences:

You can hear me, bitch? Good. I'm not leaving this hot-blooded young man because he belongs to me. I got in while he was at a brothel and his aura was open. Now I make him go to brothels all the time, and we have a lot of fun. You can't even imagine what that's like, can you, you little prude?

"It makes no sense for you to remain where you no longer belong," replied Carmen, "when a much more interesting and pleasant life awaits you. You are now in a cold, dark place where you are not happy."

Well, that's true, but how can you know that? Have you been here?

"I have helped many like you who are lost, sending them to the world where they belong, to a life of harmony and happiness that is found in the light. All you have to do is call for the light, and it will come."

What world where I belong? There is no world other than the one I left behind, and to which I'd love to return. You're telling me unbelievable things. What light? There is no light here.

After finally convincing this soul to call for the light, he said:

I'm going to try to call for this light. But if it's not there, you little bitch, I'll kill you. I will go to the light. I'm calling for it.... There it is.... I can see a glimpse of it, and it's getting bigger the closer I get.... This is something I have never seen before, and never felt before. It overwhelms me. It pulls me. I can actually feel it. Where is it coming

*from? Does it come from God? I never believed in Him.
Now I know He exists. Everything makes sense in this
light. You were right. What a waste of time Earth is
when this place of light exists. Thank you for helping me
get here. I apologize to Fernando for having bullied him
so much. Tell him he should stop going to those places
where there are so many others like me. They will get to
him. I am going to heaven. God bless you both.*

No matter how defiant a soul may be, the light comes to all
who call for it. This is how Fernando was released from his
attachment to the dense vibrations of the night life. There was
no penance for the soul who had possessed him. Once again,
we have proof that punishment does not exist.

There are cases of obsessive souls who pursue an individual
because of karmic debts from a past lifetime. Such was the
case of Rachel, a sweet ten year-old Jewish girl who sometimes,
for no reason whatsoever, behaved in a very unpleasant and
aggressive manner, and so began to attract the antipathy of
those around her. Her parents became very worried, as it seemed
their daughter was possessed by some alien power.

They sought the help of Carmen, who established contact
with the being possessing her.

*This girl you call Rachel was once my executioner, and now
I will have my revenge. She wants to be good now, but I'm not
buying it. I'm doing everything possible to make sure she's not
good, and that she suffers the consequences of her cruelty.*

Carmen spoke of forgiveness, to which the soul responded:

*What are you talking about? How can you speak of
forgiveness when you don't even know what she did to
me? She was vile and dedicated to causing me the most
suffering possible. After my death, I swore to take revenge
for all eternity, which is what I'm now doing. The things
you speak of are hard to believe. And this little girl? How
is it that she has changed so much? How does she get the*

body of a Jewish woman when before she was a male Nazi jailer? When I was imprisoned, I was stripped of everything, including my dignity and rights as a human being. I didn't understand anything. I died in the gas chamber of one of those horrendous concentration camps, naked and humiliated. I don't see how you can speak to me of a better life, or of a light I don't see, or a love that doesn't exist!

Despite his rage, this soul did eventually release Rachel, who was able at last to find peace. Her attitude improved dramatically after that.

Nothingness

If you believe there is nothing after death, then nothingness is what you will find: a thick mist of sorts that isolates you from both the spiritual and physical worlds. It's important to open our minds now to the idea of the soul's survival in order to be better prepared to enter the astral plane. This will allow our soul to feel less disoriented and will also help us be more responsible about our actions in this life. As an example, here's a communication from a soul who himself was caught unawares:

I'm surrounded by a cold fog. I don't understand what's happening to me. I didn't know what death was. I thought everything ended with the disintegration of the physical body, so I was afraid of it. At the same time, I didn't care about what I was leaving behind since I didn't know what would happen after my death. I was very selfish, always thinking only of myself and my desires. Now, in this loneliness, I've had time to think, and I feel so sad when I realize how much harm I caused. I'd been told there would be a punishment, but I don't see that either. I see only this cold fog.

We helped this soul escape his predicament, as we have so many others.

The hellish way stations of purgatory are not really places but vibrational fields produced by our own consciousness, and are therefore voluntarily chosen. The light is always there. It depends on our state of awareness whether we recognize the light or not. We are not forced into anything; our free will is ever-present. Therefore, should our mind be solely occupied with earthly interests, we will remain in the lower astral in darkness.

Throughout life, we choose either to live in darkness by doing everything in our power to guarantee ourselves a certain outcome, or to open ourselves to the light by learning to accept life as it comes. True humility is found in understanding that everything has a role in our spiritual evolution. Learning to die is no different from learning to live, in that both require our surrender to divine will; it's a letting go of how we want things to be and a faith that everything is actually as it should be.

Every opportunity, whether in the moments before death, or the moment of death, or any moment during our lives, is a chance to let go of the desire to control and to understand that this desire is based on fear, not love. Any extreme attachment to ideas, things, people or situations, is generated by our feelings of separation and loneliness. We come to earthly life to understand that we are never isolated, that we are all connected, and that our essence is love. We come to understand this as we begin to live from love, our true essence, and not from fear, which until now has governed most of our reactions.

Those with a relatively undeveloped consciousness require the expenditure of a great deal of energy to achieve detachment. Still, our attraction to He who brought us to life is stronger than the desire to be in the world of illusion, and ultimately we all go to Him. Prayers from earth and assistance from the spiritual planes help us all find release, so we who remain on earth are advised to pray and send love and rose-colored light in order to help the lesser developed souls find their way back to the light of God.

There are many disincarnate souls whose mission is to help people still on earth. Here is what one of them has told us:

We don't really require the assistance of a medium to communicate with the earthly plane. We're constantly communicating, and many humans are able to hear us fairly well. Sometimes it's hard for us to communicate because those we're helping are very wrapped up in the ego. They wish to dominate, to stand out, and to possess, and this may not allow them to hear anything beyond their own passions. In such cases, we provide situations that, though painful at times, provoke in them a positive reaction.

There are many cases wherein people act lovelessly and only for their own ambitions, and do not suffer a setback in life. Sometimes it's necessary to allow them to reach the limits of their ambition before they realize that true satisfaction will not come that way. After experiencing death, they come to know that all they lived for was hollow and of no use to them. If they let go of their attachment at that point, they have a real opportunity to see the true way.

For many, it is quite difficult to break away from the lower astral plane. Many souls remain attached to the power and possessions they once had. But as we've said before, our attraction to our Source is stronger than any other. It's possible for these souls to spend centuries, as you see it, in the lower astral, but the prayers and counsel of the embodied are ultimately successful. This is why it is so strongly recommended that you pray for the souls in purgatory because prayer generates an energy that helps free those who are stuck.

Both our planet and everyone on it are undergoing a process of evolution toward our point of origin, and this process is accelerating. The planet will go from being an elementary school where the ego learns its hard lessons, to a higher school where love and brotherhood can be achieved. This is what is meant by a "new age." As this evolution progresses, it will be easier for souls to free themselves from the lower astral because the change in earth's vibrations will draw upward those capable of seeing their errors.

It's important to know that the spiritual concepts we know on earth are actually quite far from spiritual reality. The body is like a suit of armor that closes us off from the spiritual dimension. When we descend to the material world's frequency, our memory of other planes is quickly lost. The density of this reality interrupts the fluidity of higher vibrations. If something is submerged under water, it loses touch with the outside world. If the same object is buried in the mud at the bottom of a body of water, it loses touch completely. Likewise, the dense vibrations of physical matter separate us from other realities. The physical body is like mud, in this sense, and once we have left it behind, we are better able to understand divine truths.

This is why we continue to state that no one here knows the absolute truth. When we are embodied, all we can see are glimpses. Each person can see but one aspect of the Great Truth, without being able to comprehend its totality. Even so, we must try to open ourselves to our own inner light, which is the ray of light emanating from Cosmic Consciousness, and so be able to more clearly understand all truth.

3

The Astral

~

Most people are asleep but do not know it.
They are born asleep, live their lives asleep,
They breed children asleep, and die asleep
without ever waking up.
They never understand the absolute delight
And beauty of that which we call human existence.
All of the mystics, Catholics, Christians, Non-Christians,
Whatever their theology may be,
independent of their religion,
Unanimously agree on one thing:
EVERYTHING IS ALL RIGHT.
Without a doubt, this is a strange paradox.
But the sad thing is, most people never
know everything is all right
Because they are asleep. They are having a nightmare.
~Anthony de Mello, S. J.

Whether at the level of the lower astral or that of the higher astral, those who shed the body must adapt to a new life. Our consciousness enters a state of awe as the unexpected unfolds before us. With the help of the beings of light awaiting us, understanding is facilitated, but newcomers are often defiant or incredulous and will not listen. It requires a great deal of patience and love to help the slow learners accept that their long-standing beliefs may not correspond to their new reality.

Once again, mankind's eternal problem—that of pride—interferes. Pride does not let us see our own errors, and so we rebel against what is contrary to expectation. It's sometimes extremely difficult to convince new arrivals to let go of their prejudices and surrender to the light of the Supreme Being. Still, the attraction of the Creator is so intense that all submit to it in the end.

I Don't Understand Why This Happened to Me

Marina's cancer was aggressive and her condition critical, but she refused to accept the inevitability of her death. Her youth and her desire to live prevented her from facing reality. For her, death was something entirely negative.

Jocelyn began to visit her regularly and tried to broach the subject of death, but Marina refused because it went against what she wanted. For Marina, there was only her will to live.

Marina died in a state of denial, without ever attempting to understand the meaning behind her illness, let alone her life and death. She resisted until the end because of her focus on what she was leaving behind: her family and her plans for a happy future.

A few weeks after her death, Marina expressed herself:

To just hang around here with no hope for relief is truly hell. I don't know why this had to happen to me. My life was cut short, and I had so much ahead of me. I got along great with my husband. I loved my children deeply. Now everything has been taken away from me, and my heart is broken.

We responded that neither her husband nor her children had belonged to her but rather were souls who had agreed to undergo this experience together, including the painful separation, in order to learn and to grow.

How can you say that neither my husband nor my children are mine? I don't believe it, and I refuse to discuss it anymore. I'm very angry at whomever took them away from me, and I will never understand the reason why. It seems everything I was taught was a lie. Where is heaven? Where is purgatory? As for hell, I am living it, but I don't think I deserve to. I never did anything bad, and I always believed what my religion taught me. Tell me something I can believe.

We explained to Marina how her attachments were keeping her in that unhappy place and that the light was there, but she would only be able to see it if she accepted her new situation and elected to go toward the light.

Telling me to leave my family is absurd. They are everything most sacred to me. How could I leave them? What you are saying just isn't true. There is no light here, just fog and darkness.

We continued repeating that God is love and mercy, and that she should surrender to Him.

What you're saying does give me some little comfort. When I hear you say that God is love and mercy, I know deep down that it's true, but I still can't understand the reason behind what happened to me.

"Your true life is not here," we answered. "This is merely the school we attend to learn to develop our various virtues. It would be unfair if this were the only life we had, with all the suffering and inequitable fates that exist. True life is found in the world of spirit."

I'm feeling peace. I will think about this idea that true life is not to be found in the physical world. Religion teaches that, too. You've given me a sense of peace. I will ask God for mercy. Please don't abandon me. Go on sending me love.

Over the next few days, we continued to send light to Marina. She appeared once more, and we helped her achieve her final step in letting go of the earthly plane. According to what we've been told by others who have taken this step, the sensation of accepting the light is like being bathed in love. It feels as though a wave of warmth and wellbeing has enveloped them. Since they are no longer limited by a physical body, they feel this energy far more directly than we do. Love, being the energy that unites the Creator with his creatures, helps those who receive it to self-elevate to the higher planes.

Those who have gone through this process say that, when a soul sees the Creator's light that illuminates the world of spirit, it then rises to the astral plane with which it has a vibrational affinity. There, souls are able to see with total clarity all the acts they committed during the lifetime just ended. From this perspective, there is no possibility of self-justification. Souls witness their acts of egoism and their many transgressions against love, and this may be very painful for them. This review of our life takes place in the presence of the beings of light known as the Tribunal of Justice. They are not there to chastise but rather to radiate healing energy that washes away any negativity caused by guilt. It is Justice's exalted beings, who, with boundless love, help us to forgive ourselves and understand that our errors arose from a lack of awareness. Rather than reaffirming non-acceptance and self-contempt, these beings lend us their support by helping us see what was positive in our lives and to learn from past mistakes.

People who have had near-death experiences, meaning, come back to life after being declared clinically dead, say that when presented with the panoramic view of their lives, they viewed it both as spectator and as participant. What most amazes such people is that they could feel all the suffering and joy that they had caused others. This explains the meaning of the phrase, "Thou shall love thy neighbor as thyself" because the good and bad we do to others we do to ourselves, as well.

If the astral body of the recently deceased is damaged due to a lengthy and unaccepted illness, or drugs or alcohol, or by murder or suicide, the soul enters into a period of sleep. During this time, the conscious mind slumbers while the astral body heals itself through immersion in universal energy. This is the same state into which those who have been greatly distanced from their inner light go. It's what is meant by *restorative sleep,* the duration of which depends on each individual's need.

The following is a message received from a disembodied soul who helped us better understand this process:

You cannot even imagine the beauty of the plane where we find ourselves. For you, earthly concepts must be used to describe it, but there are no words that can convey this reality. I can only tell you that the feelings of love here are sublime and that they aid our understanding of cosmic law.

The process of disembodiment begins with detachment from the mortal body. If the individual is no longer fixated on what he or she left behind, the soul immediately goes toward the light illuminating the world of spirit, and one sees very clearly the life that has just been lived. Remorse and self-judgment soon follow, but there is always the support of those exalted beings who, with enormous love, help us see when we acted rightly or wrongly.

We are then put into a state of restorative sleep to adjust our imbalances. While in this dimension, we are allowed the luxury of creating the surroundings we considered ideal while on earth, as a respite from the hardships of the life just ended.

Because there is always a latent desire to move forward, after a period of time in that illusory world, we wake up to the reality of the world of spirit. Then the real work begins, and it's incredible. There are those who apply themselves to the deeper learning of cosmic truths, to the extent allowed by their state of consciousness. This knowledge is generally retained and proves useful in the subsequent incarnation. Other souls devote themselves to welcoming and helping newcomers integrate into their new life here; still others take on the work of contacting the incarnate from here through telepathic communication.

Here is decided what will be our participation in assisting those still in the physical world. Work plans are drawn up establishing the necessary circumstances that will generate the very best conditions for the general awakening of consciousness. Our task is to properly organize the workings of the material plane such that. This is in order to correct aberrations in human attitudes by providing the incentives and circumstances that will steer human beings toward awakening.

It's not always a simple task. Individuals do not always react the way you hope. In many cases, it's necessary to try another method. This is the reason for coincidences, which many deem to be simple strokes of luck, or else cruel twists of fate. They should be understood as neither but as effects of our own actions.

Since the mind is a creative force, it creates the circumstances of our lives, drawing its images either from the causal plane or from the mental body. This means we are either coming from our internal and authentic Self trying to manifest itself, or from the mental body, which connects to the astral plane and follows the emotions engendered by it. When our desires go contrary to the requirements of our awakening consciousness, the result is dissonance that manifests in our lives as pain. Both cases have to do with the power of the mind, but at different levels. Thoughts belonging to the lower bodies are manifested in those bodies. In other words, the physical body with its material demands, and the astral body with its egocentric emotions, unlock the energy that causes selfish thoughts and those that constitute the ego. It's a cycle that feeds on the desires, needs and emotions of the lower bodies, a cycle that can be broken once we understand unity, and once the energy that comes from the higher bodies is allowed to flow into the mental body.

From here we follow the energy flow of the thoughts of those who are incarnate, and we orchestrate the necessary circumstances so that those creative desires will be fulfilled, whatever their direction. Then we help fulfill the effects of those creative desires that will assist in the awakening of consciousness. That means the creative energy that rises from the causal body.

The help flowing from our realm to yours is continuous. If we are all one continuous whole, then logically we are connected from the highest levels to the lowest. As consciousness expands, our acts are increasingly in harmony with the will of The Almighty. But to the extent that our consciousness is asleep, our actions are often disharmonious. As your older brothers and sisters, we are always watching out for our still sleeping siblings and helping them awaken by arranging circumstances that will help expand their consciousness. We may not be able to act against anyone's free will, in that his or her creative power is always present, but from the higher realms we try to discourage dissonant actions by way of stimuli that leads the person to become aware of his or her errors.

The power of the mind is vast. It constantly emits creative energy that connects with our minds on this spiritual plane and moves us toward obtaining what that mind is creating. This demonstrates how we are all interconnected, as we are all manifestations of one and the same essence. If we're able to accept that everything that happens to us is a gift helping us to learn, grow and awaken, day by day our lives will become more balanced and harmonious.

In the world from which I speak, there is neither pain nor suffering. Souls come together as a result of vibratory affinity and work in groups, helping one another. You may wonder about those souls filled with what is considered evil and egoism; how do they suddenly become peaceful and altruistic? Once outside the density of the body and enveloped in this wonderful light, their consciousness opens up, and it becomes impossible for them to act inharmoniously. This occurs once they have left the lower astral and are anywhere in the intermediate or higher astral.

Because most souls are not yet masters of the various virtues and so must undergo more experiences of the three-dimensional world, as they vibrate at that frequency they feel the pull of that world. Souls return to the physical world in order to finish experiencing everything it has to offer before continuing with their evolution at the next level of consciousness.

There are also beings who reincarnate from the lower astral plane because of the irresistible attraction of the material world. Such beings are born into earthly environments very far from the light. Often, though, through very difficult and painful experiences, they begin to let go of that low vibration and start expanding their awareness. We remind you that the actual times are purifying, and that all who do not know the light benefit from incarnating during the planet's acceleration and elevation to the next plane of consciousness.

During the current era, we are going through a change that will lead humankind to open themselves to awareness of the fourth dimension, where there is no darkness or egoism and life can be completely new. This dimensional shift will require a very long time in earthly terms but will begin in the next few generations.

There is no barrier between life and death; one is a continuation of the other in a single line of energy. Everything is energy vibrating at different frequencies. What in the physical world is understood as "life" is nothing more than a single step along the long road of evolution. When we are in the middle of this step, we think it's the only one, or certainly the most important. No doubt it does have its importance, but it's only one of many such experiences of our creative power.

Sometimes, even after souls have arrived at the first level of the spiritual realms, they continue reacting with the emotional body. In other words, they continue experiencing emotions such as guilt or anger concerning their mistakes during their last earthly experience. This delays their elevation to the higher levels. The following case is an example. Actually, it's the continuation of the case of the soul who thought he had purchased salvation.

Carmen, I have been given permission to speak to you once more to tell you what my process has been like. When I arrived in this world, after my arrogance in thinking I had every right to go to heaven because I'd purchased it. Then, thanks to the help of you and your friends, I was pleased to discover this amazing world. At the same time, though, I was angry at having been mistaken in my old beliefs.

How could I never have questioned anything when I had the intelligence to do so? My pride was deeply wounded, and despite being happy in this world, I reproached myself not only for that, but for everything that my life had been. As you know, I lived full of rancor and frustration, harassing others as a means of revenge.

You can't imagine the emotional torment one goes through when we become aware of our failings. While I was there on earth, I justified my actions by telling myself I had been my father's victim, and I thought that confessing would fix everything. I also bought indulgences every chance I got.

Thinking about all of this, I felt a sense of remorse for some time. But there are some very loving beings here who help us review our lives and learn from our mistakes. When you live in this expansive world, your understanding becomes clearer. But pride is always present, and it was difficult for me to rise to the next plane because I didn't want to admit the error of my ways. Many souls I had known in earthly life came to help me. My stubbornness knew no bounds, and it took me a long time to finally come to terms with all of this.

Now I have left my arrogance behind. The plane I am on now is where you can discover remarkable cosmic truths. It is like some higher scholastic institution where many beings gather to discuss tremendously important topics. I will remain here and continue to study these important truths while learning to practice universal love. Eventually, I will be able to rise to the higher dimensions by living in the harmony of love.

We come into the physical world to learn to better ourselves. But the real world is the spiritual one, since it is there that we consciously prepare all the experiences we will undergo in our next lifetime. In the spiritual world, plans are made and accepted beforehand as to the lessons to be learned. If the intended plan is not carried out, yet another experience will be arranged.

This means that our free will is much more active before we become incarnate in the physical world. We voluntarily choose all the circumstances regarding country, family and socio-economic status, as well as the specific sorrows and joys we will pass through in order to learn and grow. How we do, or do not, take advantage of these opportunities in the physical world is up to our free will at that time.

While souls are in *bardo*, the space between incarnations, there are many activities to which they devote themselves. The simplest is restorative sleep, which can last centuries in earthly time and is necessary to remove the negativity from those who cloaked themselves in a great deal of darkness during their time on earth. Souls who are awake can, as we have said, study cosmic mysteries and laws or help corporeal beings and newcomers to the world of spirit.

Life there is a continuation of life on earth. Or rather, life on earth is a facsimile of life in bardo. There are hierarchies there, based not on power but on vibratory frequencies. No one tries to overpower another; hierarchies are perfectly respected for they are based on the amount of light emanating from each being.

The space between human lifetimes has been investigated by several researchers, including Helen Wambach, Ph.D., a clinical psychologist from San Francisco; Edith Fiore, Ph.D., a hypnotherapist from California; and Joel Whitton, M.D., a psychiatrist from Toronto. All these doctors put their subjects into a hypnotic state and suggested that they travel to and describe the post-death state, and all subjects reported that life after death is the same as before birth. Since we have all experienced this place many times, it's as familiar to us as the earthly plane.

In his book *Life Between Life*, Dr. Whitton writes that his patients' religious backgrounds were as varied as their initial prejudices either for or against reincarnation. Yet they consistently testified that rebirth is fundamental to the evolutionary process in which we are all engaged. All of Whitton's findings agree with the information we have received through our communications.

Before beginning a new experience on earth, each soul plans the future life in detail, usually with the assistance of more evolved beings.

As an example, we quote from one of Dr. Whitton's cases:

I chose my mother knowing there was a high incidence of Alzheimer's disease in her family and that there was every possibility that I, too, would suffer from it. But my karmic links to my mother were much more important than any genetic consideration. And there was another reason for choosing my mother. The judges told me that I should experience being raised without a father in this life, and I was aware that my parents would soon be divorced. I also knew that my choice of parents would place me in the ideal geographic location for meeting the man I was destined to marry.

There was another case of a soul who decided to make herself vulnerable to a personal tragedy that would greatly change her life:

My plan was to choose a tragic event that would cause me to change my entire soul outlook during my thirties. This event would lead me to search, with whatever means were at my disposal, to find the deeper meaning of life. This is exactly what happened.

To illustrate the help of our guides and teachers in orchestrating life circumstances, we will use the real example of a woman who chose to experience material detachment in this life as a means to spiritual evolution. Despite going through many financial difficulties during the course of her life, she was still attached to certain material things. Then she was faced with her husband's loss of his job. In order to make ends meet, they had to sell something that she was deeply attached to. Since her earlier losses had not been sufficient for her to learn detachment, her guides helped by allowing more difficult circumstances to arise.

A great deal of internal work is necessary for us to learn to accept life as it comes. We must go through a long process of spiritual growth to understand that ***everything is all right*** just as it is. We must let go of the fallacy that we are the masters of our fate, and of those around us. Because we choose the circumstances that will aid our spiritual awakening, in that sense we are the masters of our fate, but from another dimension. In our three-dimensional state of consciousness, we forget this and try to change our circumstances. We are not masters of the events here on earth in the way that we would like. It's indeed possible to change certain circumstances through the power of the mind, but if this is directly contrary to what will help us learn, we will be provoking another circumstance that will be just as unpleasant as the one we wished to change.

The change of era that is coming has to do with an internal change in mankind, in which our behavior will be governed by love rather than fear. Man, having lost the sense of unity with the Whole, is guided by the fear of feeling isolated. He bases nearly all of his attitudes around the desire to control, to stand out from the crowd, and to be acknowledged, for this is what gives him a sense of security. All egocentric behavior is governed by our fear and vulnerability. The idea is that, through our life experiences, we will gradually outgrow the illusion of separateness and learn to abandon ourselves to the flow of life, holding the reins less tightly with the security derived from knowing we are being guided by the higher self.

Let us therefore turn our gaze toward our inner development and stop trying to control our outer lives, and those of others. We cannot control everything that happens by forcing life to follow the course we believe it should take. Let us accept the circumstances of our lives as they come to us. This doesn't mean that we should never take action, but that when we do and the results are not to our liking, we do not struggle and obsess because we know that there is a reason why things happen as they do.

The desire to be superior to others is very common among humans. It bothers us when someone does things better, or is more successful, than we are. Better is to work on improving our attitudes and doing our best without comparing ourselves to others. Each person has different gifts to develop, and we cannot improve those we aren't given. So stop looking at your neighbor's green grass, and strive instead to make the best of what you have. Perhaps he or she has flowers or fruit trees that are different from yours and that require a different kind of care. It is better to focus on what will make your own garden grow.

The Almighty understands everything. He accepts all our errors with undiminished love because His love is perfect. If we wish to become closer to Him, we must learn to love in that same way. The trouble is, we reject everything that goes against our personal concept of how life should be. And because everyone is different, it's not always easy to approve of what others may do. We should learn to live in harmony with those who act contrary to our expectations. We should accept them as they are, raising our vibrational frequencies when their attitudes surprise or displease us. When we learn to accept others in this way, we achieve an enormous sense of inner peace and harmony, which is the beginning of true happiness.

We have used our creative power to generate different realities in order to express ourselves variously. When we arrive on the physical plane, our creative energy becomes so dense that we lose touch with the other dimensions and remain trapped.

This three-dimensional world is described as illusory because it's merely an experimental space for our creative powers; its existence is not eternal but transitory. Once our experience of this dimension ends, the material world will fade back into its origins, as will all the consciousnesses currently inhabiting it. It's like "the breath of Brahma," the cosmic rhythm of the involution and evolution of consciousness. There is an emanation from our Creator followed by a re-absorption into Him. All that corresponds to illusion is ephemeral, not eternal. To us, it may seem eternal, but within the concept of eternity, it is only a sigh.

Our egocentric behavior in the three-dimensional world begins to dissipate as we understand that we are not separate. In this respect, our painful experiences of separation and fear in the physical world are helpful.

It is said that pain accelerates vibrations and expands consciousness. Why? Because pain is the stimulus that moves us to seek out other solutions and therefore helps us break away from illusion. Without pain there would be no spiritual growth in the physical world. Pain is also the origin of pleasure; without having had the experience of pain, we would be unable to perceive pleasure. Therefore, pain has two objectives: it gives rise to pleasure, but also, once the enjoyment has faded, it serves to motivate us to look for satisfactions more real and lasting.

We choose our earthly experience beforehand according to a specific plan, the purpose of which is to help us develop certain virtues. Regardless of whether we take full advantage of our opportunities for learning, we nevertheless learn something. The following is the testimony of a soul who can serve as an example:

I was very spoiled throughout my whole life. I had chosen riches so that I could give to those in need. But I was overcome by my ego and instead became very selfish. If we have abundance in life, we must share with others and not think entirely of our own benefit. We can never give too much, for he who gives also receives. I didn't understand this, at first. I believed that I deserved everything that was mine, and that I was master of the fates of all those around me.

Now I know this is not the case. If we are given much, it is so that we can help those in need, spread the word of the Creator, and provide moral and physical support for the sick. This doesn't mean we shouldn't enjoy the advantages we've been given. On the contrary, our essence is joy, so if we act in harmony with life, joy is what we will experience. True happiness lies in giving.

But my behavior was very egocentric. I never took into account the opinions of my subordinates, whether family or employees. I thought my opinion should prevail and be respected by all. That behavior has caused me much suffering, for here I have come to understand that one must never act against the free will of another.

I'm telling you this so you can learn from my example and understand what not to do. This wondrous spiritual plane allows you to understand the meaning of life with extraordinary clarity. That meaning is spiritual growth, becoming stronger as well as more humble and loving.

When people resist their chosen path, they fail to understand that the objective is to learn to let go of the earthly plane and become spiritually stronger. Pain is our incentive for spiritual development, and the more we accept this, the more advanced our spirituality will be. This not only helps us evolve but also allows pain to lessen, and even disappear, once we accept the circumstances of our lives.

I have been given the opportunity to communicate with the physical plane, and I am sharing what little I know. The only thing that truly matters in life is to act with love and generosity. Our selfish acts cause us great distress when we arrive here. In the name of the Creator, I am telling you that, as long as we attach ourselves to material pleasures, we will never achieve happiness. I wish I'd heard these things during my life there. Actually, we are told this in the world, but only in a superficial and unconvincing way.

We also received the following lesson about generosity:

Generosity is a form of detachment, and envy and greed are its opposites. Envy is attachment to what others have. It springs from the desire to possess everything, to have every quality, and wishing to be superior to others.

Generosity means giving and sharing what you have. It means not desiring everything for yourself, but rather wishing that others may also enjoy what you have.

Greed is the need to keep everything for yourself, to not share anything: neither your money, nor your time, nor your talents. This interrupts the energy flow of abundance, which results in very serious emotional imbalances. It also prevents loving energy from enriching us and those around us. Why? Because love is unity and therefore non-exclusive. Impossible to encapsulate in a single person, it is expansive by nature. Being an energy that unites all of reality, it does not recognize separation.

Generosity goes hand-in-hand with love for it gives whatever it has, of its person, its time, and its talents. It delights in the wellbeing of others and does not shut itself in. It is unification, union, and unity.

Everything one experiences in life is geared toward the awakening of consciousness, including death. Every death carries an implicit lesson, both for the person who undergoes the process and for those left behind.

I Held onto Life and All it Offers

When Felipe died, he was at the peak of his life, professionally and emotionally. He had spent years taking care of his ill wife then had lived as a solitary widower before finding love and companionship with his new wife, Emma. For her, as well, this new marriage was a contrast to her unhappy and conflicted first relationship. Not long before Felipe died, we saw him at a social gathering. When the subject of death came up, he refused to even acknowledge its possibility, despite his already being so close to it.

Shortly after we heard of Felipe's death, we sent out our thoughts to him, and he communicated with us through Carmen. According to our guides, when you think of someone, making contact is as easy as dialing them on the phone. In Felipe's case, especially, though we did not know each other well, his desire to communicate with the physical world was strong:

*Our meeting wasn't a coincidence, and I realize now that
I was given the chance to meet you for the assistance you
might later provide. Now I am truly desperate. I neither
desired, nor was prepared, to leave the world. I had finally
found a partner whom I loved, and who was a fine person.
Despite an economic crisis, my business was going well.
When you brought up the subject of death, I didn't even
want to hear about it. I held onto life and all it offers. To
me, death was something far away and highly improbable.
Yet it came without warning at the best moment of my life.
This was extremely cruel, and I cannot accept it. I don't
know if there is a God, but if so, I don't understand why
He would give life only to take it away.*

We told Felipe that he did not belong here anymore, and that
God does not take life away, but rather allows us to be in this
world long enough for us to learn an important lesson. When
our learning on this plane is finished, it begins on another, and
so we leave our body. As always, we counseled him to trust and
to go toward the light.

*I don't want to see a light. I want to go back to the place where
I was. I was happy there, but I don't know how to go back.*

"This earthly life is not the true one," we replied. "It is only
a school. A beautiful world is waiting for you. There, true
happiness, love and brotherhood reign, if you'll only wish for it."

*What you say sounds very nice, but not very real. If it were
true, I would already be seeing this wonderful world of which you
speak. I don't want to see a light, as there is no such thing. Thank
you for your good intentions, but they are worthless. Goodbye.*

A few days later, Felipe contacted us again and transmitted
the following:

*I don't understand what happens to me whenever I'm
with you. I can clearly feel your thoughts of kindness
trying to help me. But I regret to tell you that I don't
believe there is a light. There is nothing here but cold and*

darkness. When you send thoughts of love, I do feel a sense of relief. I feel very alone here. I don't see anyone, only fog and darkness. Sometimes I catch glimpses of what I've left behind, everything that I can no longer have, and this makes me very sad. You say there's something different and better than what I have now. Where? I don't see it. I feel warmth when you talk to me, and that is a comfort. Keep sending me what you call love. Maybe I will see that something exists beyond this cold and gloomy dungeon.

"The comfort you feel when you sense our love, is to show you what you will find in the light, only multiplied a million times over."

Felipe wanted to believe us, but whenever he thought of his Emma, it would set him back. He wanted to see her. He asked that she join us in our efforts to free him. It was not an easy wish to fulfill. Emma, as do so many others, had a difficult time believing in the afterlife and in communication with the departed. But, finally:

It's true. None of us believes in these things while we're on earth. I never thought about what would happen after death. We think we'll go on forever, and that death is something to not think about.

"We do go on forever. You are beginning to understand that death does not exist."

You say we go on forever, and I'm beginning to understand that, as obviously I'm still alive. Maybe I would believe it if Emma were to say it.

Meanwhile, Jocelyn had sent Carmen's book, *El Camino de Regreso* (*The Way Back*), to Emma, with a note that suggested she read the chapter on death. We heard from a mutual friend that Emma did not wish to read the book, thinking it highly unrealistic. Hearing this, we didn't ask her to be with us during our next communication with Felipe.

The following week, however, we received a call from Emma, who asked to see Carmen. Our mutual friend had told Emma about our communication with Felipe, which convinced Emma that it might be worth exploring the possibility, so we invited her to attend our next communication. Time passed, though, and Emma did not come.

During that entire period of time, we continued sending light to Felipe, and at our next meeting he again communicated through Teresina:

I feel such an intense pressure in my chest that I can barely speak. (Felipe had died of a heart attack.) *There are many beings helping me here. I don't want to meet with you now because Emma isn't there. She promised me she'd come, but now it seems she doesn't want to.*

Later, Emma did finally arrive, and she confessed her doubts. Her tardiness was a kind of self-defense. Our guides told us that Felipe was surrounded by beings who were trying to help him. He refused, however, to hear anything that did not refer back to the world he had just left, and to his beloved wife. Felipe had agreed to hear us only if Emma was present, and when she had not come, he had withdrawn. In his anger, he continued to feel the same pains his body had felt at death, as his mind had not progressed beyond that point. But, thanks to the light we had constantly sent to him, he agreed to communicate with us again.

"Why do you keep yourself wrapped up in that self-chosen pain?" we asked. "There is a lovely world that awaits you. Trust us."

I don't believe you. There is no truth.

"You have shut yourself in. Your pain is only in your mind. Why won't you call for the light?"

There are many things that keep me attached to this world. I didn't leave my bank documents in order. I'm worried about my son; we weren't very good friends. My son always saw me as an authority figure. And why hasn't Emma come? Why is she pulling away from me?

At least our guides let us know that the pain in his chest was disappearing.

There is something I don't understand. I see spheres of light that surround me and try to push me forward.

"They are the beings of light that are always around you. Let yourself go with them."

They're taking me to a tunnel. I'm afraid. Everything is yellow, and I can't feel the ground. The strings have me tied up.

The strings mentioned by Felipe were his mental attachments to everything he was leaving behind, which were so strong that they had materialized as actual tethers tying him down.

Then a message arrived from our guides:

We are helping him leave. He needs you to propel him forward with rose-colored light. Its feelings of warmth and safety will allow him to move forward. He is beginning to let go.

Emma arrived at that delicate moment and, convinced by the veracity of Felipe's channeled words, she joined us in sending him light. Soon after, we received a final message telling us that Felipe had broken his bonds:

He is overjoyed at seeing Emma. He has left his mental prison and begun to go toward the light. He has only stopped for a moment because he wants to tell his wife how much he loves her, and to ask her forgiveness for not having left his affairs in better order. She must forgive him and understand that this is the experience she is meant to undergo... He is already heading toward the tunnel, where it will be easier for us to help him... He has already freed himself. Don't worry about Felipe anymore.

It had been very difficult for Emma, as well, to accept her loved one's absence. She had felt helpless. She'd once told us that he had protected her and always said that he would never leave her. A few months later, we met with Emma again, and she told us she often saw him in her dreams. Then we received the following message:

Dearest Emma, do not resist the lesson you chose for yourself before becoming incarnate: emotional detachment. Your life is meant to be a tool for learning this. Though painful, it is the stimulus you need to let go of the human attachments that have summoned you again and again to the three-dimensional world. If you are able to pass this test, the problem will be over and done with. Please know that Felipe is already in the light. The purpose of his visiting you in your dreams is to tell you this. He loves you just as much as before, even more, but hopes you will pass this test and that he will meet you again here, with a love that is no longer possessive but universal.

I Can't Leave My Precious Things Behind

It all began when Adela was very young and her grandmother gave her a beautiful, antique porcelain cup and saucer. Adela was meant to use it, but a warning from her mother—"It's a very fine and fragile piece; take care of it"—made her very protective. The glossy cup, edged with tiny blue flowers and featuring an elegant, slender handle, fascinated her. It was rare for a child to be so careful, and soon her aunts joined the familial chorus: "Adela is a very mature child, with such refined tastes." So she was given another cup, a small vase for her bedroom, and when she was a teenager, a tea set "for when you get married, for your collection." Adela never asked herself whether her interest was real or merely an assumed pose, but by the time she married, her collection filled several shelves, and her proud husband continued the tradition. Adela, who at first enjoyed the smooth feel and the patterns, became obsessed with acquisition. She filled shelves with vases, plates and one-of-a-kind pieces. Just as others collect jewels or postage stamps, Adela scoured antique galleries and specialty shops for one more special object, each more exclusive, and more expensive, than the last. Esthetic enjoyment turned into something darker. The collection grew, and with it, Adela's anxiety. Jewels can be insured, stamps can be hidden in albums, but porcelain owes part of its charm to its fragility, its vulnerability. No one was allowed to open the glass doors of the cabinets, let alone touch their precious contents. Adela's son, Juan Carlos, felt that he lived in a museum. The first words he learned were, "Don't touch; it can break." Once he ran into the living room, banged into the tea table, and caused what seemed a monumental catastrophe. The potbellied sugar bowl, filled to the brim with multicolored cubes, shattered, scattering its contents over the shoes of his mother's guests. The scolding was terrible, but it was his mother's screams and tears that disturbed him the most. He cried, too, in great, gulping sobs, unable to deal with the magnitude of his crime. Afterward, he was properly consoled but warned, "You must be careful. Don't run in the house. Don't ever go near the china. Never be careless."

Due perhaps to subconscious reasons, Juan Carlos married a woman quite opposite to his mother. Yolanda was practical and interested in doing, rather than having, and Juan Carlos finally felt comfortable living in a house where objects were simply to be used. When his mother died, Adela bequeathed her collection to her only child. Yolanda, terrified of the crystalline avalanche about to descend upon her home, suggested selling it, or donating it. To her surprise, Juan Carlos, who had always made fun of his mother's obsession, objected. Perhaps it was out of filial affection, or a sense of guilt, but the boxes of china filled the floor of the house, waiting for custom-made shelves to arrive. After installation, Yolanda hated the way the walls looked. Before, they'd been elegant in their simplicity. Now she preferred to walk past without looking. The delicate objects in their wood and glass prison gave her a feeling of unease. Yolanda wasn't alone. The maids came up with any excuse to not go near the china cabinet, and soon dust covered everything. Yolanda's daughter, who since childhood had used the dining-room table for her personal desk, began complaining, "Mommy,

Grandma won't let me do my homework." Yolanda thought it her daughter's imagination, but the girl insisted: "I feel her behind me, Mommy. She stares at me. I can smell her perfume." Finally, Yolanda, ever the pragmatist, contacted us through a mutual friend.

The day of our visit was dark and rainy. The wind rattled the trees in the garden. We arrived early and were shown into the living room to wait for Yolanda. We were surprised that the room was cold and noticed that the windows were all open. Yolanda arrived at that moment, and we asked her if she could close the windows, as we were freezing. "Forgive me," she said. "This house is always like a refrigerator because Dora, the cook, keeps everything open. She says it will make the night spirits go away." Yolanda explained what was happening in the house, and we understood at once that there was a presence there.

Carmen began receiving the following messages:

I'm told I should no longer be here. But where can I go if my precious things, which took so much effort to collect, are here? Being in a place where there's nothing more than darkness, and from which I can only see what I have left behind, fills me with despair. While we are in the world, we're told that after death is either heaven or hell, but that isn't true. There is only this nothingness, this darkness, filled only with nostalgia for what I have left behind. If I want to, I can see that world, but I cannot materialize in it. No one can see me or hear me. Now I understand that the place of death is blackness and loneliness.

As always, we explained that she needed to go toward the light, where a beautiful life awaited; that her attachment to her objects, now of no use to her, was keeping her chained to the darkness. We always have free will, and we are not forced to do anything we do not want to do. If our wish is to continue thinking about what we have left behind, that in itself will prevent us from seeing the light that emanates from God, who is love and mercy. The only thing that matters in life is to act from love.

Why didn't I hear any of this during my life? I don't understand how you know something that no one else does. If it's true, then why is it not taught by religion? To act with love isn't easy when all of life is based on selfishness. You look out for yourself, or you are eaten alive. Now you're telling me that love is the basis. How can I completely change from one moment to the next? To look at our misery is not pleasant, and I'm beginning to see everything I did without love—but how do you expect me to change just like that?

We continued speaking to Adela and sending her loving energy, which, after some time, resulted in her beginning to approach the light. She finally let go, telling us:

I didn't realize that heaven is so close, but now I do. Death doesn't exist. You go on to another life, which depends on your own will. Our attachment to what we've left behind confines us to a black space, and when we open ourselves up to the light, the light is there. It's wonderful. It is love. It is peace.

When souls are attached to a particular place, one need only speak to them with love and convince them of the infinite mercy of the Creator, and the new life that awaits them. At the same time, we pray, and this energy helps them let go of the past.

Some time afterward, Yolanda gratefully let us know that peace had been restored to her home and family.

The Landowner

For a long time, Patty had been searching for the house of her dreams. However, every time she was close to deciding, she would hesitate. It was either slightly too big or too small; it didn't have quite enough light, or there was no garden for the children, or no study for her husband. She was never quite satisfied. Finally, one day her realtor took her to a golf community in a relatively new suburban neighborhood. Where cows had grazed not long ago, now grassy lawns and trees created an ideal setting for houses surrounding a small artificial lake. Patty was excited. It was what she had always wanted: the tranquility of the country, with green grass and trees all around, but with the advantages of the city. When she took her husband, Daniel, to see it, he was a little skeptical. The house seemed neglected and in need of work. Patty was able to convince him, promising to take care of everything herself, which she in fact did. Over the following months, she worked hard, sometimes transporting the materials herself and supervising the workers. One of the workers who lived nearby told her she was moving into a haunted house, but Patty didn't take his remark seriously. They soon moved in, and her husband made her feel proud of her accomplishment. It had taken time and a lot of work, but finally the family had their dream home.

Their joy did not last long. Daniel's business, which had always been successful, was suddenly failing. Orders stopped coming in, and an audit revealed that his administrator had mismanaged the business. Despite the endless hours he devoted to trying to save his company, he was forced to declare bankruptcy. Depressed and irritable, Daniel neglected his family. Patty, in turn, had many sleepless nights, as she felt that her relationship with her husband was falling apart. She was soon questioning her emotional stability, as during her bouts of insomnia, she sometimes heard terrifying screams from a male voice. She would get up and try to discover where the screams came from, but always in vain. No one else in the house heard anything. Patty began to notice a disturbing pattern: the screams seemed always to herald a serious conflict or misfortune. In one instance, her eldest son crashed the car, resulting in disproportionately high repair costs. Then her daughter became ill with a recurring virus that forced her to stay out of school for a year. At other moments, Patty would receive bad news from her family, or there would be a serious conflict with Daniel.

Desperate, Patty sought out Carmen through a mutual friend and explained the situation. She could not understand why only she could hear the screams. Carmen explained that Patty probably had psychic abilities that other family members had not developed. We went to her house and began the customary ritual: flowers, candles, incense. When we tried to use our recorder to play Gregorian chants, though, it didn't work. Patty substituted her player, then her children's, but we were unable to make any of them work. Carmen soon received the first message:

This is my house! It was taken away from me by those fucking farmers who took over my land. I've been here since I lost my body, watching people come and go, intruding upon what used to be my property, and I hate it. This is why I scream out of frustration. I don't know what else to do. It's very dark here, and I don't know where else I can go. My only companions are other disembodied people in this same situation.

We sent him thoughts of love and urged him to find the light.

What light? There's no light here. I see your candles, and I see that you're surrounded by light. What does that mean? You do bring me a bit of peace. Who are you?

We explained why we were there and described the help we could give him.

I feel very good when you speak to me. Also, when the woman who lives here prays, I feel calm. For a while, I no longer want to cause her harm.

We told him of the life that awaited him and the way he could ask for it.

No one ever told me these things. All I ever knew was to fight for my land, but when your body is taken away, that fight becomes useless. You tell me I should ask God for light, but I never believed in Him. I still don't.

We continued praying, speaking to him of God and sending him rose-colored light.

> *God's name shines bright. I don't know why, but when you mention Him, I see a sort of radiance, and this makes me begin to believe that you may be right. But maybe I don't deserve what you say awaits me. I was very pig-headed and cruel during my life. I killed more than once. I think my victims may be the ones surrounding me in this black hole where there's nothing but hate and resentment.*

At that moment, we received the following message from our guides:

True love is that which does not judge, that surrenders itself to trust in God, that forgives itself and forgives others. Our essence is like that of our Creator. It is love, mercy, harmony, and happiness. Our purpose is to discover that essence that resides in each of us.

It required several sessions to convince this recalcitrant spirit, but his final message was the following:

I'm leaving. I apologize to the woman who lives here for all the harm I caused. Now, without me, this house will be filled with the light that you have brought.

And so it was. Patty later confirmed it.

Each time we help those who remain attached to the physical plane, we receive enormous support and direction from our guides. Here they speak of this process:

> *How is it that after having acted so negatively in life, a soul can suddenly go toward the light?*

What you must understand is that the light is our natural habitat. From it we have come, and to it we return. If, during our experience of the physical world, we cloak ourselves in darkness, it is only transitory, as it belongs to the illusory world of the physical plane. When we return to the world of spirit, if our desire is to see the light, that light will envelop us, and our consciousness will open to it as much as our spiritual evolution allows.

It's not necessary to be "good" to be in the Creator because, even if you have acted against universal harmony, His will was behind that behavior. All beings ultimately return to their Source because His plan is so wise that it attracts even the most wayward back to the fold. Everyone who leaves the path of love ultimately returns to it, guided by the very effects of their waywardness, which are conceived so that one always comes to understand that love is the only path to true happiness.

In our current times, there is more and better communication between the physical and the astral, thus incarnate beings can help those stuck in the lower astral plane If they have been there for a long time, it's increasingly difficult to reach them from here. They don't listen to us, yet they are able to make contact with you. It will not be easy if they have spent centuries in that confused state, but with love, prayers and patience, you will succeed.

4

Living and Working in the World of Spirit

~

The mind is its own place, and in itself
Can make a heaven of hell, a hell of heaven.
~ John Milton

Death does not exist; we are as eternal as the Fountain of Life from which we came. Our true home is the world of spirit. We come from there to make decisions in the physical, then we return home. While in the physical world, we find ourselves in unexpected situations and among those with whom we agreed pre-birth to share experiences.

In the spiritual world, where true life exists, there are different levels where souls reside, depending on their vibratory frequency. We also advance while in physical form, for life is about evolving until we can return to our origin. We come to this worldly dimension to experience darkness, which we are truly not, and each experience in the physical world serves to bring us a step closer to the discovery of our true nature.

The work we do after physical death and passing through the light, is quite varied and highly productive, as we will now see in messages received from souls residing on the spiritual plane. It's clear that more advanced souls constantly help those who are less advanced. Here, one such soul recounts his experience, step by step:

After passing into the light, I realized there was, in fact, no punishment awaiting me. There was only God's infinite love filling me with joy. I saw my parents and other loved ones come forth from the light with loving expressions such as I had never seen on their faces on earth. This filled me with happiness, and I went toward them. They received me with so much love, and explained what awaited me. First, I had to go through the process of self-judgment. During that process, I saw every detail of my life pass before my eyes. I was filled with remorse. It was like being back in my physical body except that I felt all the pain I caused others. During self-judgment, you see, with heavy sadness, all the opportunities you wasted during the life just ended, and this serves as an important teaching. In the next step of the process, you enter a period of rest during which your astral body recuperates. Once this process is complete, you pass into the first plane of the spiritual world, where you can create anything you ever wanted during your earthly life. This is the origin of such concepts as Nirvana, or being surrounded by a hundred virgins, and so forth. Personally, I chose to be a Parisian woman with money and jewelry, going to parties and to the theater. That's what I would have liked to be, so I repeated it as it was an experience I has already had in another previous life, so I lived it as though it were real. When I grew tired of this fantasy, I was taken to the second plane, where I opened my consciousness to truths I had known in past experiences but had forgotten during my most recent incarnation, distracted by materialism, laziness and ego. I chose not to return to earth because I feared having a similar experience; instead, I decided to continue my evolution here. I worked tirelessly, receiving newcomers, and radiating love to all those around me. I found myself among beings of light who helped me continue to self-elevate, and after a lot of effort, I ascended to the third plane, where I find myself now.

Such messages are often very similar in content, yet every individual has particular experiences and impressions:

When I entered the world of spirit, I was delighted to find unexpectedly beautiful things composed of materials that do not exist on earth. I saw incredible buildings, and flowers of extraordinary color and radiance, the likes of which have never been seen in the physical world. I did not rebel when faced with my own ignorance, as many do. Rather, I chose to be thankful to God for so much beauty. I stayed in that first place for some time. I created a house that would have been my dream home on earth, and invited friends over to share my joy. I was very happy. You can find friends you knew on earth here. We recognize each other by our vibrational frequency. I don't know how exactly to explain it, but when you come across an entity, you know exactly who it is. What form do they have, you might ask? Here souls select an appearance they are comfortable with, either from their most recent life on earth, or from some other, or they may simply take on any form that resembles the human body. It matters little because it's by their vibration that we're able to recognize them.

I still felt a lot of guilt. When I was finally able to free myself of it, I felt a sense of freedom that you can't imagine. An indescribable, magnificent light opened just before me and carried me to the first plane. My family was waiting for me at the threshold. I had never before felt so much love emanating from them. They took it upon themselves to explain what awaited me, and even stayed with me while I grew accustomed to my new surroundings.

I enjoyed that level, but after some time I needed something more, so my family members returned to show me the path to the next level. The path is nothing more than a process of recognizing our failures, accepting that we are not perfect, and desiring to move forward in our evolutionary process. Once we reach this point, we pass on to the second plane, where we find schools that teach interesting cosmic lessons, which we study while reviewing the Akashic records. All this serves as preparation for our next experience. The second plane is amazing! Our understanding expands, and our joy knows no bounds. From this level, we try to help those still incarnate, which is always possible. My family members were, and are, just souls like any other, and they have played different roles with me during various lifetimes. We all help each other, but we each must take responsibility for our own personal spiritual evolution.

Here, our love is sublime. Negative feelings fade and soften but are never completely eradicated. This is why we require other lives, other experiences that will help cleanse us of our negativity. Most of today's humans returned to the physical world from one of the many layers of the second spiritual plane. Once we have completed the work of the entire second plane, we continue our ascension to the next. This is done through great spiritual concentration, and by deciding to completely leave behind the ego.

When we reach the third plane, we must make a decision. We can choose to either reincarnate or continue our evolution in the world of spirit. I am now trying to ascend to the third plane, but it's not easy. Pray for me, as prayer does help.

It's interesting to learn that our prayers help souls wherever they may be. Prayers convey an energy that ascends to where a soul resides and helps them advance toward their final destination. We are told that the form adopted by the soul on "the other side" corresponds to that being's self-thoughts. The astral body, along with the other higher bodies, is the energetic mold of the physical body, from which it separates at the moment of physical death. The astral body is composed of mental waves, so its form is the result of the person's thoughts. Our appearance, created by our mind, is even more self-reflective after physical death. If, at the moment of death, we are still very attached to the way we presently look, we will continue to appear as such. If, however, we see ourselves in the bloom of our youth, then this will be our form. Thus, when we catch sight of the spirit of a dead person, we see them as they think of themselves.

The following information was received from a soul already on the third spiritual plane:

Evolution continues in this marvelous world, and this is what we try to do once we're no longer attracted by the three-dimensional world. Once we ascend to the higher planes, a whole range of possibilities opens to us. For one, we can choose to return to the three-dimensional world to help those who are lagging behind, but you need a lot of love and courage to do this. You can also help those stuck in "hell," who remain wrapped up in false pride. This is also a difficult task because the vibrational frequency of those souls is very low, and the density and negativity is not easy to cope with. Another option is to simply remain in this state of beatitude for a while, sending uplifting messages to those who are incarnate. A lot of help is always being sent from here to those in need.

Different realities correspond to different vibrational frequencies. The first astral plane is very close to the earthly frequency and therefore similar in its reality, yet enhanced. Just as in the physical world, we create our own circumstances, yet our creative power is magnified in the astral, allowing us to easily create what we wish for. The following describes this facility:

The first plane of the spiritual world is quite similar to earth but much more beautiful. The ocean is a magnificent color, while trees and flowers radiate with a light unknown in the physical world. There are buildings of all types because those who arrive here are free to construct whatever they desired during their time on earth. Everything here is a creation of mind and last as long as they remain in the mind of the Creator. Souls on this first spiritual plane meet and share their experiences, but attachments to physical life slowly fade, allowing souls to continue their ascension. Those of us who have already gone through this process assist others in understanding universal truth.

There are those who resist accepting concepts that they did not ascribe to during earthly life. For example, my brother, Edgar, found it very difficult to leave behind all that had been his life, and especially to admit that, despite his intelligence, he had been mistaken. I had no problem with that since I had never been interested in religion, nor had I really believed in all the dogma. I had followed and respected religious tradition though many of its doctrines made no sense to me. Out of laziness, I never really tried to seek out other answers.

What I personally found difficult was letting go of the power and comfort I had attained on earth. This attachment made it painful to release myself from the earthly vibration. Once here at the second astral level, though, I was amazed at everything I saw, and it was easy to leave behind the fantasy world of the first plane. It's our arrival in the second astral that marks the beginning of our true life in the spirit.

On this second plane, we study universal laws, cosmic truths, the meaning of creation, and the practice of unconditional love. It's much easier to practice that here, since this plane does not have earth's adversarial atmosphere. However, our ego has not yet been completely eradicated, and we are told that going back to earth would eradicate it completely. Though we do advance here, it's a much slower process than on earth. There are those who stay here to continue their evolution, but without reincarnating and going through the obstacles of the physical world, it's a lot more difficult. This is why it's so important to reincarnate.

I'm going to tell you something about abortion, which is not, in fact, murder since the soul is not continually within the fetus. During physical gestation, the soul comes and goes, gradually preparing its home in physicality. Abortions do impede a soul from becoming incarnate when it has a pressing need to do so. This is why religions proclaim that we should have many children. This, however, is often exaggerated. We believe that one should have as many children as one can effectively support and educate. Having more children than one can care for is not recommended, as the souls may be born into an inharmonious environment. We are currently trying to influence religious leaders to encourage responsible parenting.

When we live our lives very attached to our beliefs and arrogantly refuse to let them go after death, we are unable to advance from the first astral. That was the case with Edgar, who could not continue his ascension because he remained caught up in old beliefs:

I am in a difficult moment because I want to be able to remain in this magnificent world, yet there is a force that drives us to continue to elevate ourselves. We achieve this by searching for the truth rather than remaining tied to the way we are accustomed to think. I'm so happy here that I don't see why I should look for anything more, but I'm advised to continue with my evolution, as they call it.

Should I believe that we are part of God and must discover our divinity, as they insist?

I don't know what to do. I think I still haven't gotten rid of my pride, and I don't really want to let go of what I have believed, though I do realize that things here are not what I'd expected. I'm going to try to be more humble and flexible in the way I think. I will open myself to further instruction and help.

Carmen spoke with Edgar a few days later, and he reported:

You've finally convinced me that there are realities I never dreamed of. I now see that, even in the world of light, I have remained arrogant and unmoving. I am now going to begin the journey toward the truth.

Guilt is one of the main reasons why a soul becomes stuck. The following case involves someone who committed suicide. After rising to the first plane, he was unable to continue with his evolution because of his guilt at having caused so much pain to those around him. This is what he told his wife through Carmen:

Patricia, I need you to know how much I love you, and how sorry I am for having acted as I did. I was in despair at not being able to leave behind my misguided attitudes, my foolishness, and my unhealthiness about facing reality. Your wanting to leave me was very painful, even though I understood that you were exactly right.

Please forgive me for having been a coward and a fool. I took my own life in a moment of madness, and when I saw what I'd done, I was filled with anguish. I was rescued by beings of light who brought me to this wonderful place that, in truth, I don't think I deserve.

They tell me that God welcomes everyone with love, no matter his or her errors.

I have been given an opportunity to talk to you now, that I may ask for forgiveness for the pain I inflicted on you. My feelings of guilt are keeping me from moving forward on this magnificent path. I anxiously await your forgiveness, and your prayers, that I may continue forward. I will prepare a place for you here, as I did not know how to properly do so on earth.

Another reason a soul may be impeded from ascending is when that soul is excessively mourned by loved ones, who continue to call to him or her mentally, saying how much that person is missed. This creates an energy cord that ties the soul down. Below are two cases in which deceased husbands communicate with their grieving widows:

My beloved Caroline, I haven't left. I am with you always because I see that you are unhappy. I feel, though, that it's time for us to part. I cannot continue my ascension to the higher planes, and you cannot carry on with your life, with so much sadness hanging over you.

In the place where I am now, I've realized that each of us must live different experiences in order to learn certain virtues and to correct old imbalances. This allows us to rise on the evolutionary scale.

Life in the physical world is but one stage in a long journey, and we are there only for a very short time. We will meet again, here in spirit, which is our true life. Be patient, my dearest. Live the life you've chosen for yourself to its fullest. The time we experience on earth passes very quickly, and I'll be waiting for you here with all the love I've always had for you, and will always have.

The other:

My love, I must see you happy. Your pain is holding me back, and I cannot ascend any further. I have come to understand many things here, including the choice we made together before I left the physical world; that we would separate soon, in order to grow spiritually.

My death was a blessing in that it was quick and painless. The only true pain was seeing you suffer and leaving you behind. But now I'm in a magnificent world where everything is love and harmony.

I have work to do here, but it's difficult for me to let go because I see your suffering. Believe me, a life full of satisfaction is awaiting you here. We made an agreement that this pain would make you stronger and lead you on a deeper quest for God.

I have been given this opportunity to explain that, if you let go of the energy that's keeping me chained, I'll be able to ascend to higher planes. From there, I will be able to help you more effectively. God does not send us hardships. It is we who accept them as either hardships or instruments to help ourselves rise and return to our Source. If you only knew how wondrous this life is, you'd know that the difficulties we undergo there make sense and are worth the pain. Be brave, and have faith that everything will be all right.

Once we have experienced all that the physical plane has to offer, and we have let go of it, we continue our evolutionary process on higher planes.

As we have seen in these examples, the life that awaits us is simply magnificent.

5

Reincarnation

~

To cultivate exterior knowledge
Without cultivating internal knowledge
Inevitably creates the values
That drive mankind to destruction and pain.
~ Krishnamurti

*I*f we contemplate the wonders of creation—how each
particle of energy combines to create different types
of matter; how the laws that govern the universe
demonstrate a profound wisdom—we cannot come to
any other conclusion but that we were conceived by a
superior intelligence, and that our existence could not
have been spontaneous. A universal order exists that
cannot be easily denied, governed by an unfathomable
force far superior to anything we can imagine.

Another obvious truth is that everything evolves. At
the beginning of the physical universe, different forms
of matter gave way to celestial bodies. Then, gradually,

what we call life emerged. First in plant form, then in animal form, and finally as human beings, possessed of a more evolved consciousness that allows self-awareness.

Evolution, therefore, is an indisputable fact, even if we do not know its future. Each of mankind's sages has spoken of this in their own way, but all agree on one thing: we are returning to our origin. All who devote themselves to seeking answers in the spiritual world come to the same conclusions. Admittedly, they all interpret their experiences according to their own abilities and criteria, but in essence each tells his or her own version of the same story.

When discussing evolution, we inevitably come to the topic of reincarnation. Many do not believe in it at all, and those who do believe have many interpretations. What is the truth? Actually, all interpretations possess some version of the truth, but as we've said before, humans cannot understand the vast complexities of creation. Three-dimensional consciousness cannot penetrate a process encompassing seven dimensions.

As we open our consciousness to other levels, we begin to better understand the creative process, the reasons behind events, and the universal evolutionary process.

As a follow-up to the above lesson dictated by our masters, we would like to add our own voices to the discussion of reincarnation. This controversial idea holds that man is born on earth over and over again until he becomes aware of his own divinity. This theory is very old but until recently was a well-kept secret. Only the highest-ranking religious authorities knew about rebirth because it was believed most people were not yet ready to properly understand.

Now such Eastern religions as Buddhism and Hinduism teach the doctrine of reincarnation, while Western religions generally deny it. Yet this is far from a new theory in the West. The early civilizations of northern Europe were convinced that reincarnation was a reality. The Druids held reincarnation as a basic tenet of their religion. Originally, the Greek word for *education* was the same word that meant to extract something already known. According to Plato, "Knowledge easily acquired is that which was obtained in an earlier life, which is why it flows back so easily."

In its beginnings, Christianity accepted reincarnation. Fathers of the primitive church who spoke of it included Clement of Alexandria; Origen, who is considered one of the greats; and Saint Jerome. In the fourth century, Christianity was institutionalized as the official state religion, and it was then that opposition to reincarnation began. At the Council of Constantinople in 553 AD, under the rule of Emperor Justinian, belief in reincarnation was declared heresy. Justinian drafted a formal decree banning belief in "the monstrous repetition of birth." Then he went after the "heretics" (from the Greek *hairetikos,* which means "free to choose") who ascribed to "Origin's heresy." Reincarnation probably was thought to provide human beings too vast a panorama. Man would have little motivation to fight for salvation during one of many lives on earth, so church authorities declared that we have only one opportunity to determine our fate for all eternity. This made it easier for the new alliance of church and state to manipulate people with fear of punishment for not following established norms.

Throughout history, there have been groups of Western mystics who maintained a belief in reincarnation. One such group was the Cathars, who were cruelly persecuted in the thirteenth century. The systematic persecutions carried out during this time were almost successful in eradicating the belief in reincarnation in the Western Hemisphere. Nevertheless, such groups such as the Gnostics, the Rosicrucians, the Theosophists, various alchemists, and others, retained their belief in reincarnation, though they lost prestige as a result.

A belief in reincarnation isn't required for our evolution. It is pivotal, though, in helping us to understand many things.

How else do we come to terms with such inequities as different life circumstances, different fates, different states of awareness, and instances of extreme suffering? Without reference to reincarnation, it would seem that life punishes some of us while rewarding others.

All of life is about growth through overcoming obstacles. Every individual is at a precise level of consciousness, and experiences differ from person to person because each is conceived very specifically to teach certain virtues and to open up the creativity within each of us.

The mind is creative and generates the various planes of consciousness, including the physical one we now share, and creates, as well, every moment of our lives. Why do we create pain, suffering and horror? Because we need to experience all the feelings that characterize life on the physical plane in order to mold our soul. When an artisan creates a beautiful object from metal, the metal must first be put to the fire to soften it, then it is placed in a mold. Afterward, the cooling metal can be encrusted with precious stones. In the same way, our souls need to know pain, limitation, error and virtue, in order to complete their understanding of the physical world. Every one of us ever to have been here, has chosen to experience this place.

The problem is, we become so involved in our own creations that we forget it's all an illusion. We become attached to certain stories and re-create them over and over. The result of that attachment is that we manifest ourselves on this plane again and again. Because of the law of cause and effect known as karma, we return each time in a different form. We create the circumstances necessary for our energy to be expressed with sufficient clarity that we no longer need to return. Accepting one's karma means understanding that injustice does not exist. Inequity and misfortune are merely learning aids.

Each life on the physical plane is likable to an academic cycle. Our higher self designs the curriculum for our improvement, and to rectify distortions due to egocentric behavior during the course of our evolutionary process. Before we begin any new incarnation, we choose the conditions necessary for us to learn the appropriate lessons during our next academic cycle.

It's important to note that karma is not punishment, as is often believed, but rather an opportunity to repeat necessary lessons until we've accomplished our goals. In this school, everyone ultimately passes the test. There are no failures; we just need to review certain lessons until fully assimilating them. We may attend as many classes as we wish. Once we have achieved understanding, the universe will put us to the test. Sometimes these tests seem quite hard, but they are all exams that we will, in the end, pass.

Before each incarnation, we agree to temporarily forget our true origin, so as to fully enter into the lesson. It's as though a curtain falls separating us from the world of spirit. This forgetting is necessary in order to discover faith, which would be impossible if everything were always clear to us. Sometimes the curtain becomes more transparent, enabling us to see more cosmic truth. These flashes of insight serve to confirm our faith, which after all should not be blind, but rather borne of personal learning and a deepening personal wisdom.

In the world are beings at many different levels of evolution. This does not mean that some are better than others; we all have the same amount of spiritual light. The difference lies in the degree to which each of us has purified our bodies through non-identification with the ego. We are all learning different lessons, thus some focus on issues concerning material things, while others focus on issues with success and recognition. The most evolved among us are working on non-judgment and acceptance of everything in the scope of human experience.

We need to experience everything, the unpleasant along with the pleasant, as the former is what tempers us and makes us stronger. Pleasure is merely an incentive enabling us to continue with our struggles.

How can we understand that we are all equal when some of us act with love and harmony, while others choose to violate themselves and others, and even the planet itself? This is something we can only understand in terms of "light" and "absence of light." Those who act negatively do so because they are connected to an emotional and mental body filled with darkness; in other words, where the ego rules. That being said, the internal reality of these individuals is not evil; it's pure light. After many lessons, this light eventually manifests. We should not judge these beings but instead understand that their actions are borne of fear and ignorance.

All human actions are interconnected. Even the most inharmonious act can serve to teach the lessons of detachment, compassion, and non-judgment. If these troublesome people didn't cross our paths, how could we practice acceptance and charity?

Learning is everything, and we're always exactly where we need to be to learn what we came here to learn. The more attentive we can be to what life is telling us through the situations we face, and the more accepting we can be, the better we will understand the meaning of existence.

We must trust in the life experience that we are offered, and work with love, courage and faith. Let us be compassionate toward ourselves and others, knowing that we are loved beyond all comprehension. We are never alone; each second of our lives, we have the support of our angels, teachers and guides.

We need to understand that we are in an evolutionary process that will take us back to our origin. How it happens is not important; what matters is our method, which comes down to a single word: *love*.

In each of our manifestations on this plane, we are following the law of karma. Once we have sufficiently understood all our lessons, and we have exhausted our interest in the many illusions of the three-dimensional plane, the higher self ascends to the next stage of its evolutionary journey.

Each time we disrupt universal harmony, which is love, through egocentric acts, we elicit a counter-effect that helps us understand the error of our ways. This is karma, or the law of cause and effect. We are then given an experience that teaches us the correct course of action. When our behavior is distorted, the repercussions are inharmonious and serve as an indicator that our act was unwise. This should not be perceived as a punitive act initiated by the universe. It's just an effect of a cause that needs correction so as to reestablish equilibrium. Following is a message from a soul who spoke to us from beyond:

Life in the world of spirit is true life, but we cannot understand this while immersed in physical matter. The heaven described by religion is nowhere near the truth of what heaven is. Here, our joy is infinite, harmony abounds, and work is gratifying; neither pain nor disillusionment exist. Why then do we choose to leave this behind and reincarnate on earth?

Our existence here is wonderful, but the attraction toward the Source that gave us life and individuality is always present. It's because of this attraction that we feel compelled to move forward, and we know that there is no better school than life on the physical plane, and that we need to understand it completely. In other words, we must go through the full range of experiences in order to earn graduation to the next plane. Since it was our own will to manifest in physical matter, we must exhaust physicality until we want nothing more of it. While on earth, we find it difficult to understand why we would choose to suffer and face diverse hardships. We must understand that the perspective of this dimension is unique. From here, we know that suffering and hardship help us break free of the attraction of the earthly plane. As long as we continue to vibrate in its range, earth will continue to hold an irresistible attraction for us. We choose to suffer because it raises our vibrations and helps us detach from a plane that often traps us with illusory pleasures.

Here we may no longer feel attracted by those false pleasures because we've come to understand their futility, yet we may still need to learn forgiveness, patience, or humility. We are always surrounded by harmony here, so we may be unaware that we have not yet learned to love profoundly, or that we do not know how to be generous, or that we still haven't attained true humility or patience. All of these virtues must be fully developed, and because we live here on a kind of floating cloud of wellbeing where there are no physical needs, we do not have the opportunity to fully develop those virtues. Only through lifetimes on earth can we truly learn. Because the environment there is so adverse, our learning can be very deep. It's really the only way to put our evolution to the test.

Of course here, too, we can continue to evolve. But there are certain learning experiences offered only in the physical world.

Suffering, even when we don't accept it, speeds up our rate of vibration and helps us detach from the physical world. Why does it raise our vibrational frequency? Suffering is provoked by something that is not in accordance with our desire for wellbeing, and that desire is what makes us cling to this dimension. Suffering raises us above the earthly vibration by opposing it.

While suffering is part of worldly life, it is more precisely a consequence of the disharmonies generated in the world. This consequence tends to restore the balance and is therefore said to be of a higher vibration. When there is a tendency toward disharmony, something moving in the opposite direction is needed to restore balance. In this sense, suffering carries a positive, or harmonious, charge.

The Non-Existence of Space-Time, and the Totality of Self

From the point of view of the three-dimensional world, the reincarnation process is a sequence of temporal events. From the perspective of the higher dimensions, however, where eternity is an unbroken present, everything is seen as happening simultaneously.

Reincarnation, as we think of it in the world, exists in terms of time, and does not exist in terms of no-time. A soul can manifest itself through different bodies, in different lifetimes, at various moments and simultaneously. This idea is difficult to grasp for those immersed in time, so we'll speak of reincarnation simply as various human experiences of the higher self, each of which helps it to evolve.

Space and time are an illusion of the third dimension. In reality, they do not exist as we perceive them.

What is no-space? It finally comes down to a sense of oneness. Because we are part of an indivisible whole, there can be no distance separating us one from another. Where there is no distance, there can be no space.

Distance is not real in terms of higher consciousness because it only applies to three-dimensional reality, i.e., illusion. In the physical world, beings tend to withdraw unto themselves, losing awareness of their oneness. When they feel separated, they actually are separate, but the vast, insurmountable distances they perceive are only the result of their unevolved consciousness. In other words, the universe is exactly as we see it. But what if we believed that we could travel to Venus just by thinking it? That is what beings on other planes of consciousness do.

Our consciousness has existed since the very beginning, given that it is a spark of that extraordinary power source we call God. We came to be at the moment He decided to liberate those particles from Himself. When individual experience began, individualized consciousness began creating different planes on which to manifest (the physical world being but one), leaving a portion of its consciousness in each. The self that acts in physical reality is but a part of the Total self that expands and grows with all the experiences gathered from various realities.

We should not feel daunted by knowing how vast we are. We are multidimensional beings, and the part of our totality that is active in the physical world is merely a fragment of who we are. Our work is to elevate our consciousness from this plane where we don't understand our true reality, in order to increase our creativity and act with a broad consciousness based on all our experiences. Other facets of ourselves are living other experiences in other realities, contributing their creativity to the totality, as well.

Declaring that reincarnation does not exist causes a great deal of unease. It *does* exist, but not as a sequence of events in time. As we've seen, time as such does not exist. In its greater expanse, life is a continuum, and we experience everything at once. The various lifetimes are experienced as occurring at different moments, but they are in fact concurrent.

The concept of no-time and simultaneity is beyond present human comprehension. When describing reincarnation as the process of a single entity undergoing various experiences is to say that the Total Self is having these experiences simultaneously through its different personalities at different points in time. When we perceive these other lives while under hypnosis or in meditation, it's probably due to our contacting the Total Self. We might imagine the head of an octopus receiving multiple inputs absorbed through various tentacles in order to fully experience the underwater world.

In a similar way, the higher self splits into various personalities in order to learn and experience everything the world has to offer. Once the higher self has exhausted its interest in the three-dimensional plane, it moves to the next dimension. There it investigates what that world has to offer, gradually integrates the learning achieved through all its lifetimes, then re-integrates its various personalities until it reconstitutes as what it was in the beginning: a spark of divine light returning to its Source.

It is better to view this process, not in terms of time, but in terms of movement, as the Creator is continuously moving and expanding, expressing Himself through His creatures as would the conductor of a great orchestra directing his magnificent symphony.

This divine music runs through everything, even the shadowy illusion that is the physical world. Everything at every level has order and harmony as its goal. If life sometimes seems disharmonious, there is also a counterpoint, an undercurrent whose purpose is to restore balance. The individualized consciousness within each human being wishes to experience disharmony, disunity, and non-love—but a healing impulse is also set in motion in such situations, reestablishing equilibrium, and universal harmony. This divine order is what is meant by karma.

Modern people tend to reject reincarnation and the whole idea of living a series of lives in different bodies. From the perspective of no-time and no-space, reincarnation in fact, does not exist, for the whole notion is based on misunderstandings. How can we comprehend no-time and no-space while living on a plane constructed of time and space? It's like asking an ant to describe the outer landscape from inside its tunnel.

We must try to understand that everything happens at once, and that the same soul experiences various personalities and lifetimes concurrently. It can be said that the same great soul is absorbing every possible experience through different personalities, depending on what must be experienced in order to learn the different virtues that bring us closer to God.

If everything occurs simultaneously, why do we experience events as occurring sequentially?

If we accept that we each agreed to incarnate in the third dimension, then we must accept, too, that we agreed to experience time. The recovery of cosmic consciousness needs a process. People speak of involution and evolution, of emanation and absorption of the divine energy, of moving away from universal consciousness then returning to it. The factor of time is implicit in all of this. How, then, can everything be simultaneous?

If simultaneity is understood as movement and eternity as a continuous present, it can be seen that the past still exists in the same way that the future is already determined. This is not the same as determinism because free will exists, and the decisions we make cause events to flow one way or another. The future pre-exists in the form of probabilities. When, in a given situation, we make a particular decision, our choice produces an effect that already existed as a probability. Had we opted otherwise, the result would have been the activation of another pre-existing probability.

This idea is not easy to grasp, but we are not puppets. The divine gift of free will is always at play. Think of a fabric. When we choose one direction in life, that decision is woven into the fabric and ultimately leads to harmony if we make choices that are direct and efficient. All of this implies a process of learning, thus a sequence of lives within three-dimensional consciousness. Ultimately, it's about the totality of self undergoing experiences through its multitudinous personalities, as in the example of the octopus with its several tentacles. If one tentacle creates disharmony, another counteracts that effect through a counterbalancing experience. The result is a properly woven fabric.

As long as we are immersed in physical matter, we cannot completely comprehend these abstracts. But we can sense them intuitively, and thus know both the timelessness of, and the impermanence of, life.

Here we include a message from our teachers:

Being individuals, that is, having been endowed with individuality, does not mean that we are separate from others, but only that we have unique missions and purposes, just as each cell has a role in the perfect functioning of the human body.

Our own purpose is to awaken the consciousness of those still asleep, while at the same time expanding our own consciousness. We are on a journey that will take us back to the Source, a journey of several stages. We are still concerned with the first stage, the physical world, which we must leave behind by our own concerted effort.

On the long journey of evolution, those of us who have chosen to venture into this shadowy labyrinth must undergo multiple experiences to discover the way out. Each experience teaches us different things. After each experience, we are able to judge where we made good decisions and where we went wrong, which prepares us for a subsequent experience.

It's hard to understand how, if everything is simultaneous, we can prepare for a "subsequent experience" in the physical world. Speaking from the perspective of sequential time, between each life experience is a rest period during which the higher self chooses when and where its next experience will take place, and with whom. Describing the same process from the perspective of no-time, we would say that the higher self simultaneously splits into different personalities that compensate for each other and work together to reestablish the balance lost upon entering the darkness.

It is at this point that the totality of self raises its vibration and leaves the third dimension behind, continuing its ascension toward the higher planes that will lead it to merging completely with God.

The Concept of Reincarnation in the Third Dimension

Given our three-dimensional consciousness, simultaneity is a difficult concept. So let's discuss reincarnation as a series of steps in time.

Since the very beginning, there has been a desire within consciousness to express in physicality. In order to truly know all that this world has to offer, we must undergo many different experiences. Through them, we make full use of our creative capacities. Everything is conceived so that we may learn to love and mature, to acquire the virtues that will help us to manifest our essence. and then to detach ourselves from the physical plane and rise above it.

When approaching the plane of physicality, we create an allegorical play through which to act out our drama. This explains the purpose of illusion, for theater is impossible without it. Using our God-given creativity, we play various roles of beings inhabiting the physical world. In this way, the Creator manifests Himself very specifically, while safeguarding the outcome of the play, limiting the chaos of unrestrained cause and effect.

We ask ourselves; why is it necessary to go through the process of duality? The answer is, this is the method we chose to experience different states such as emotions, limitations, and triumphs, and to discover our ability to create every circumstance we require, and so understand our true power, which is extraordinary. When we submerge ourselves in the refractive waters of duality, our emotions are needed to differentiate between what is helpful and what is not. Our emotions are not the core of our being, but within the experience of duality, they help us to navigate.

We decided to experience our "what is" by living within "what is not" and so understand the fullness of our beauty, harmony and happiness. We needed painful experiences to be able to appreciate happiness; disharmony in order to know harmony; and the limitations of the physical world to appreciate our limitlessness. The problem is that, once we are in the illusory world, we become so attached to it that we have difficulty leaving and returning to infinity where we belong.

The human being requires many varied experiences in order to elevate his or her state of consciousness. The soul rests after each immersion in the physical plane, as we always become very distracted here. The ego fully emerges in physicality, which process is necessary in order for us to affirm our individuality, but eventually we cross the line into separatism. At that point, discordant thoughts and behavior break out, creating the distortions that become illnesses of the soul, very difficult to cure. These illnesses are spiritual in nature but are expelled from the energy system through illnesses manifest in the physical body, which are dissolved through pain. Alternatively, they can be assuaged by our becoming aware of our pathological patterns, and correcting them.

In many cases, a significant amount of pain is required to stimulate the awareness of error. Repeating the same behavior over and over again gains us nothing, for the more distortion we experience, the deeper into error we sink. Eventually, this sinking may itself be enough to cause us to react. Every situation in the physical world offers multiple options. If we choose a path that causes us to sink further into distortion, later we will find ourselves in a circumstance that offers an alternative to distortion. Habitual errors, often expressed as behavioral vices, often pass unchanged from one life experience to another, and we may find it necessary to hit rock bottom before finally reacting.

While incarnate, it's very difficult to see our own distortions. Once free of the body, we can see our patterns quite clearly and, in light of that, choose our next experience with the objective of being healed.

Passing the test means emerging victorious over the attitudes that tie us to the earthly plane, and this is achieved to the same extent that we let go of our selfish desires. As long as we are concerned with standing out in the crowd, possessing more than others, and controlling everything around us, it will be difficult to pass our final exam, and the physical plane will inevitably draw us back to it. Our goal must be the greater happiness for which we were created, attained by living in harmony with the infinite.

In all that we experience throughout our innumerable incarnations, free will is a constant. We exercise it quite forcefully before each new experience in the flesh, establishing all the circumstances we need to carry out the tasks we've set for ourselves.

Before each lifetime, we choose the exact conditions we need to accomplish our learning goals, including the physical vehicle and the individuals who will be closest to us. We may choose the latter because of bonds we share from prior experiences, either because there are issues still needing resolution, or because we simply wish to work with them. Dr. Helen Wambach has documented numerous cases of individuals who, through hypnosis, recounted such planning sessions. The following cases appear in her book, *Life Before Life*:

> *When I think about the purpose of my current life, I realize that it consists of establishing new relationships with people I hindered or harmed in previous lives. I am perfectly aware of the fact that I am supposed to help my husband, an alcoholic in this lifetime, because in a previous life I behaved very badly toward him.*

And:

> *In a past life, my mother was a nun and my father a gambler. I chose to experience those extremes, both to help them achieve their destinies and to achieve mine.*

Life in the spiritual world is our true life, though we cannot understand this while immersed in physical matter. Our experiences on earth are meant to help us evolve and obtain wisdom, but it is in the spiritual realm that we are truly alive.

The following speaks to this evolutionary process:

> *We have voluntarily descended to the physical world in order to experience material life. But we have become so involved in this experience that we have forgotten our divine identity, and our minds remain trapped in the three-dimensional world.*
>
> *Our limitless thoughts became limited, imprisoning us, though voluntarily, in the limitations of physical*

matter. What remains is for us to become aware of our divinity and progressively shed our limited way of thinking. This is achieved through meditation and by progressively letting go of this place where our hearts are trapped.

Why can't we let go of our desire for power, for standing out, for special recognition? Why can't we stop identifying with our bodies, our families, our positions, and our belongings? All these things bind us to physicality, compelling us to return again and again.

Now there is an opportunity for change. The ideal time has arrived for opening our consciousness to what we truly are; for liberation from limitations caused by our limiting thoughts.

Once again we, your older brothers and sisters, tell you that we have freed ourselves and that it wasn't difficult. You need only focus your attention on the limitless, leaving behind that weary plane where every possibility has been exhausted. Nearly all of you have gone through every experience the flesh has to offer: power, pain, sickness, joy, wealth, destitution, intelligence, foolishness—all of them with the objective of stimulating your creativity. This world was created by us, and its true objective, to give glory to the Creator, has already been accomplished. The time has come to leave it behind, to move on to the next plane of consciousness where our creativity can find greater inspiration.

Our help will become more evident day by day. There will continue to be want and anguish in the world, but these stimuli are necessary in order to spark detachment from that plane. A new era is approaching in which humankind will take a great step forward in its evolution. May the Creator be with you.

The cases that follow are of two people who chose illness as a learning method:

We are not Meant to be the Center of Attention

At the age of thirty-nine, Sophie began suffering from amyotrophic lateral sclerosis, otherwise known as Lou Gehrig's disease. It's a terrible illness that causes progressive paralysis resulting in death. Sophie was a young wife and the mother of two children just entering adolescence. Of course, it was very difficult for her to accept her illness. She tried every means possible to find a cure, but to no avail. Instead of wallowing in self-pity, Sophie gradually came to see her illness as an opportunity for growth, and that she could find true healing in forgiving both herself and others. She learned to view her life as a different kind of adventure that was neither better nor worse than that of others, simply different. Throughout, Sophie never gave up hope. But she believed that, even if her body did not heal, her efforts would not have been a waste because she would become a better person, more full of love and peace.

Throughout the six years of Sophie's illness, and as her paralysis progressed, Sophie experienced every emotional extreme, vacillating between angry rebelliousness and willingness to accept her circumstances as they were. She wrote:

> *Discovering that my illness was an opportunity for growth has been a slow and difficult process. But this has been a school of life where I've learned to seek inner peace, to live in the present, to leave behind guilt about the past and fear of the future, and to not try to change others, etc.... I know that inside me, and every one of us, is a being of light, complete and unchangeable; we just have to learn to bring that reality into focus. A friend of mine says that we're all tuned into AM radio, seeing and judging at a low frequency, but that we can learn to tune into FM and see with the eyes of the spirit and the heart, focusing only on the luminous in ourselves. It's easy for me to see myself as that complete and luminous being, but when I hear myself try to speak, or when I try to pick*

up something from my lap and can't, I see that there's a part of me that's falling to pieces. Even so, I believe that healing is closer than we think; perhaps a part of it, at least, is in our hearts.

Jocelyn began visiting Sophie a year before her death, hoping to help with the process of acceptance. When Carmen met her two weeks before she died, she was completely paralyzed and unable to speak, but the expression in her eyes was of immense peace. What most impressed us was the light that emanated from her person. That day, two of her friends joined us in meditating and sending light to Sophie. During the meditation, a wave of loving vibrations suddenly washed over us and moved us to tears. We received the following message through Carmen's writing:

Blessed and praised be The Almighty who allows us to comfort the suffering. If it is Sophie's lot to live with great suffering, it is because she so chose. She wanted to make as much progress as possible in her evolution during this lifetime, which marks the end of an era. Her family members agreed to incarnate with her as an impetus that would help them, as well, to open their own consciousness. Do not despair. You must understand that if your physical vessel is no longer of use, with each passing day, the soul becomes more transparent and the spirit more clearly manifest. This is what you wanted when you came to this experience, Sophie, and it is what you have achieved. We eagerly await you and will happily celebrate your arrival. Your year of intense schooling has been successful, and you will graduate with honors. We are each given what we ask for, and so it has been with you.

Two weeks later, Sophie died in perfect peace and with total acceptance. Before her family passed along this news, Carmen was told:

Sophie's painful process has ended, and she is being warmly and lovingly welcomed here. Her earthly experience was very positive, and she made great progress in the opening of her consciousness. Now she needs to help those left behind to understand the reason behind the difficulties of her life because it was a learning process intended for them, as well.

Two months later, when we were with Sophie's mother and husband, the following was communicated:

At the end, my body, which was no longer of any use, was there, but at least half of the time, my soul was here. My material life was difficult, and I sometimes rebelled against the obstacles I faced, but that life was the one I had chosen before birth. I needed a powerful lesson, and I accepted it. I know that I caused those around me a great deal of pain, but that was also agreed upon beforehand, and everyone was able to learn much. Here, that kind of lesson is called "an intensive course," and so it was for my husband, my mother, and my children.

If I was the instrument of their pain, it's because they agreed to it, and I can only tell them that the pain will be worth it a million times over once you arrive here. You can't even imagine the happiness in this place. The purpose of my speaking to you is to tell you that, though it's true that we suffer on earth, that suffering turns to glory once we arrive here. It isn't that our Creator is cruel, nor that the more we suffer, the more he rewards us. Those are misunderstandings. His love and mercy are infinite, and if he allows us to suffer, it's to temper prior inharmonious behavior, thereby opening our consciousness to the only means of reaching Him, which is love.

If she who is writing this was placed in my path, it's because her message gave me the final push that helped me let go of the material world. It was through the immense love of the beings of light who spoke through her, that I was able to take that final step toward the light. I can only tell you that when I arrived here,

I received a heavenly welcome. My wish, and my advice, is that you open yourselves to new concepts with neither prejudices nor rigidity. Nobody knows everything, nor does anyone possess the absolute truth. We are working on our evolution toward the Creator, and that work is highly personal. As our consciousness evolves, we need to entertain increasingly profound concepts. Remaining stuck out of fear will not help our spiritual progress. We need to understand that each stage corresponds to a different explanation of the same truths. You are now ready for more profound concepts.

Before her death, Sophie had researched the causes of her illness with a friend, Vicky, a psychotherapist who had helped her a great deal through her process. Both believed diseases to be essentially psychosomatic, and Sophie was convinced that part of the reason for her physical condition was the abandonment she had suffered as a child. One year later, while I was with Vicky, Sophie communicated this through my pen:

Vicky dearest, I am in an incredible place where there is neither pain nor negativity. The real message of my illness was that everything we go through in life is about learning to let go of our arrogant ego. If at first I thought my illness resulted from the abandonment I experienced as a child, it was because my ego wanted recognition and validation. There was quite another reason for my illness. I needed to understand that we're not meant to be the center of attention but to be giving to others. My illness was instrumental in teaching me humility and patience, which I had resolved to learn during that incarnation. Yes, it was difficult, but how great is the reward here! My advice to you, Vicky, is that you continue to try to convey to others these concepts of eternal life and progressive eradication of the ego, which is what separates us from our Creator.

Why Me?

When he was forty-two, Hugh died of lupus, a devastating illness from which he'd suffered for a decade. Jocelyn visited Hugh a few weeks before his death because she knew he was despondent. During her visit, she passed along Sophie's story, hoping it would help Hugh better understand the reason for his own situation. Sadly, it had no effect.

Hugh died a month later. A few days later, he communicated the following:

> *I'm told I can communicate with you, Jocelyn, though I don't understand how this can be possible. When you came to me with the story of the woman who had accepted her illness, and had in fact chosen it, I didn't believe a word. But I now see that I can communicate from here with certain people, such as the one (Carmen) who is writing, and I realize that what you told me wasn't a lie. When you said that I wanted to die, let me tell you, I did want to go because what I was experiencing wasn't living. I didn't want to go on deteriorating, but now I feel very confused and angry concerning what has happened to me.*
>
> *Why me? Why this? Why now? I read only the title of the book you gave me, but that was enough to push me deeper into desolation and anger. I can only tell you that what I've found here is horrible: darkness and cold. I expected either to find nothingness, or to have heaven offered to me. I had always followed the precepts of the church, though I can't say that I believed everything it taught. Tell me, do you know what's going on? How can I escape from this prison?*

We replied: "Dearest Hugh, it is your own defiance that keeps you in the darkness, just as it kept you from accepting your situation in life. Your anger is what keeps you from seeing the light and the wonderful life that now awaits you. You only have to set aside your rebelliousness and ask to see the light, and you will be free of your prison."

You say I didn't accept my life, but I accepted my poverty and my awful parents. The only thing I couldn't accept was my illness, which cut short my life at its very peak.

We said, "Our experiences are the incentives we need for growth. Nothing is coincidental, and illness is one of the means we choose to purify ourselves and advance spiritually."

I don't understand when you say that illness and hardship are stimuli for learning. Then why isn't everyone presented with these difficult situations? Don't tell me it's because you're one of God's favorites that these things happen to you.

We explained, "We are all in a process of evolving toward God. We came from Him in order to return to Him with full awareness of our identity. To this end, we experience every kind of circumstance: poverty and wealth; health and sickness; love and indifference; and the whole range of human experience. We agreed beforehand to undergo many lives in order to progressively understand the true meaning of love, which is our essence."

I don't believe that I've lived before, or that I'll live again. Where do you get these stupid ideas?

We said, "It doesn't matter in the least whether you believe in reincarnation. The only thing that matters is that, through these experiences, we learn to accept our circumstances because that's the attitude that will eventually free us from bondage to the ego."

Don't talk to me about acceptance! I can't help the anger I feel at my horrible luck. I've lost what I loved most: my family. I can't accept that, and I won't!

It took a long time for Hugh to release his anger, but through great effort, he finally began to see the light and finally let go.

Illness

The cases of Sophie and Hugh are clear examples of how illness serves as a stimulus for spiritual growth. Illness develops from disharmonies in the astral body or emotional body. Our emotions are often negative, rising from our desire for control or recognition, or from our insecurities or our lack of faith. Such emotions work against our sense of unity, creating energy blocks that impoverish our bodies, especially the astral body. When the astral body's reception of energy is negatively affected, the result is a series of distortions that begin to manifest in the physical body. Even severe illnesses such as cancer or AIDS actually act as detoxifiers, in that spiritual toxins are eliminated by way of such diseases.

We are told that we choose the body required for a specific learning experience. If we are not ill, it doesn't necessarily mean that we are free of disharmonies. Perhaps they will be expelled in a future experience, or they are being neutralized by a loving and harmonious life. What sometimes happens is that, because of our egos, we don't accomplish what we resolved to do. Thus, sometimes we see very disharmonious people in very good health.

When we agree to discharge a lot of karma during one existence on earth, the result is often one illness after another. This is merely a cleansing process that will end when we've solidified our understand that we were created to love. We must develop humility, as well, letting go of our control over our lives and those of others. Necessary, too, is the development of inexhaustible patience, meaning total acceptance of whatever happens to us. We must learn to surrender to the flow of life rather than struggle against it. Suffering will not come to an end until we see that illness is a means we chose to eliminate our disharmonies, and until we accept it as a means to learning love, humility and acceptance.

Adoption

Adoption is another life experience that many choose in order to learn certain lessons. For someone unable to bear children, adoption may be chosen as compensation for errors in other lives, such as the abandonment or mistreatment of one's children. Meanwhile, a woman who gives up a child because she's unable to care for it, may be practicing detachment. As for the adopted children themselves, their experience of abandonment may be necessary to counteract inharmonious actions in other lifetimes. The adopted also have an opportunity to learn unconditional love and gratitude toward their caregivers.

Our teachers provided the following counsel in the case of a young mother whose circumstances forced her to give up her daughter. This deep loss stimulated compassion in the adoptive mother, along with guilt for her own happiness, compared to the real mother's anguish:

When a woman becomes pregnant at a very young age and is unable to provide a home for her child, it's preferable to give up the child for adoption, thus giving happiness to those unable to conceive.

This option is also better for the baby, and the mother must realize that her child will be happier in a home full of affection and support. As for the mother's grief, this is something she herself chose in order to cleanse her karma. The result will be spiritual growth, and later she can have a family if that's her desire.

The biological mother of an adopted child should take comfort in knowing that her child is cared for and happy, and that she is not presently ready to take on the responsibilities of being a mother.

We hope these words bring solace to the one now grieving her loss, and comfort to the one who has chosen to adopt.

Homosexuality

Human love is the desire to reunite with what we have separated ourselves from. In other words, what human beings seek out in terms of earthly love, is a bond with another soul to assuage our feelings of separation. We can achieve it momentarily, but that indefinable sense of lack returns. What we're really longing for is none other than our ultimate destination, reunification with our Creator.

It's normal to feel the need to avail ourselves of human love, as this emulates cosmic union. It doesn't matter who it is, or their particulars. We need experiences of union to remind ourselves of our wholeness, as we feel incomplete within the duality of the third dimension.

Gradually, the need to feel complemented by another human, diminishes. When we come into more intimate contact with our true nature, we experience true fulfillment, true unity. Then we no longer need that other person.

If gender exists, it's because we need to experience both aspects of being human. Duality is a part of everything, including our higher self, so we must experience masculinity and femininity, assertiveness and passivity, and so forth. The current state of humanity does not recognize and honor the deep unity between them.

Homosexuality is a difficult learning method because it's uncomfortable to have a sexual preference antagonistic to what is generally expected. The pre-life decision to experience homosexuality can have different objectives. In some cases, it is to overcome the desire to be accepted by others. It may be simply to transcend the suffering this condition entails, which may include guilt, or non-acceptance of self, or rejection by others, or the absence of a family, or the absence of a steady partner, or just a different life from what was expected.

As an example of the above, a soul may wish to transcend the need for recognition by others in order to learn true self-esteem. It's important to know that our sense of security depends not on the opinion of others but on profound self-acceptance. Choosing a personality frowned on by society provides a rich experience of rejection and its attendant pains. If we can learn to transmute that pain into unconditional love toward ourselves, we can discover the true happiness depends on nothing and no one. Guilt, in particular, can be a very intense form of suffering, but we endure it in order to develop self-acceptance.

The following is a message from one of our guides to someone of this inclination who felt guilty and sought counsel:

Don't torture yourself with guilt. Put that aside. You're experiencing something you chose before incarnating in order to learn several things: self-acceptance despite non-acceptance by the world; compassion towards yourself and others; and non-judgment. Do you see all that you set out to accomplish?

When you arrive here, you'll realize that the soul and the spirit are genderless, and that we choose our sexuality in order to learn and experience different aspects of human behavior.

And now a message from a soul who went through this experience end is now in the light:

I'll tell you about my experience when I first arrived here. The first thing I felt was fear of punishment because I was convinced that I had sinned in a big way. You know the social programming you carry with you? That doesn't go away when you die, or certainly not at first. Many people I'd known on earth came to help me see the light. It was a long time before I listened to them because I was very stubborn; our character defects tend to remain after we've left the body. It wasn't until I finally saw the light and entered this wondrous world that I understood that my homosexuality was neither good nor bad; it was just one of many situations we can choose when we incarnate.

Today there are many instances of that particular choice. I'm told it's because humanity wants to transcend the need to experience gender and return to our original androgynous state. This will be achieved once we've transcended the dualism of the third dimension.

It's a powerful experience to discover that you're homosexual, to suffer from AIDS, and to experience abandonment by one's family, by society, and perhaps by one's partner, as well. The agony of this experience can be a powerful motivator to look for answers inside ourselves and grow closer to God. Unlike other diseases, AIDS carries a social stigma because of its association with homosexuality, and this becomes a very painful overlay. The presence of this illness in our world is a powerful call for compassion and love, rather than prejudice and blame. It should call into question the way we typically judge those different from the norm.

Every human desires to experience a deep bond with another. When a heterosexual romance turns out badly, we may be attracted by the idea of a same-sex relationship. These experiments are part and parcel of the soul's evolutionary process. The soul longs to regain its sense of oneness, and so it restlessly seeks this in relationships with others. It's true, too, that some heterosexuals experiment with same-sex relations in a search of more intense pleasure. As with other experiments, the result is a lesson learned. In this case, the lesson might be that happiness is not to be found in satisfying the senses but in rediscovering one's true essence.

There are souls who choose an alternative sexual preference in order to avoid sexual enmeshment altogether, instead using that primal energy for spiritual development, and for helping others in a similar situation.

This test is particularly hard because it's so difficult to resist one's sexual inclinations. Some such individuals enter monasteries to escape temptation, just as many heterosexuals do, and many are successful in putting their sexual energy to spiritual use. Many others simply follow the dictates of their inclinations.

There are also cases of people who refuse to accept their gender because they chose the opposite gender in many prior incarnations and have become accustomed to it. These are the ones who, when faced with a trying situation such as a domineering mother or emasculating father, take refuge in memories of their former gender and flee from the current one. The purpose of experiencing life as both a man and a woman, is to develop different aspects of our divine potential. When we incarnate many times as the same gender, we must eventually incarnate as the opposite in order to develop the full range of virtues.

Being a hermaphrodite is a choice, as well. This condition results from a defect occurring at the moment of conception. The challenge, as in the case of homosexuality, extends to the parents, as well, and may be related to their struggles accepting that they produced a child who is "flawed" and different from everyone's expectations.

Each gender has a unique energy that tends to complement its opposite, which is why there will always be a certain void in homosexual relationships. This doesn't make them bad, merely incomplete, since there is no exchange of strongly polarized energies, and that can be hard to accept.

None of the aforementioned sexual situations are, in themselves, good or bad. They simply are, like all the circumstances we pass through. None is an end unto itself. Rather, each is a learning method leading to self-knowledge and the cosmic truths we have talked about over and over again: love and the awareness of our innate wholeness, which are really one and the same. The particular method used to achieve this expanded awareness isn't important; what's important is simply getting there.

Below we examine the case of a soul who found it very difficult to overcome the burden of homosexuality, which of course he himself had chosen. After this man's death, Carmen was approached by his daughter, who had endured a lot of difficulty and cruelty with him. She felt that her deceased father wanted to tell her something:

At last I'm allowed to speak to you, my child, and to tell you how sorry I am for having treated you and your sisters, as well as my wife, the way I did.

I've just listened to all your complaints, and you're right. I was very cruel to you because I never accepted my homosexuality and, as a result, hated myself and was angry at everyone. To hide my sexual identity, I pretended to be the opposite. I was a big ladies' man, and not in a very respectful way. I even tried to seduce my sisters-in-law. I never enjoyed being with a woman. In fact, I found it disgusting. This created tremendous conflict in me. Now I realize that I should have accepted my predilection from the beginning rather than make everyone around me suffer.

I did not Deserve That Horrible Disease

This is the case of a soul who lost his way after dying of AIDS. Jocelyn had visited him at the hospital during the final days of his illness, when he was feeling extremely angry and depressed. Not long after his passing, we received this message:

I'm still in a lot of pain, even after leaving that useless body of mine. I did not deserve that horrible disease just because I loved another man and didn't know how to love women. It isn't our fault that we aren't attracted to the opposite sex, and I don't think it's a sin. So why this punishment? What kind of god conceives such cruelties? Now I'm in despair at finding my way in this cold, dark place with no one to help me. I've heard voices that told me to talk to you, Jocelyn, and that you can help me. But how?

As with so many others, we explained that he only needed to ask to see the light. We also explained that his illness had not been a punishment but an opportunity for learning, and that only he interpreted his situation as sin and punishment. As soon as he opened his mind to God's love, he would experience light.

That part about the light I don't believe. You're telling me very, very silly things. Where is the much-trumpeted love of God if he allows pain as intolerable as what I just suffered, and am still suffering? First I experienced the unhappiness of being marginalized because of my sexual preference. Then I suffered the abandonment of the man I loved, who when I got sick ran away as though I had the plague. And you can't imagine how my family treated me. They, too, abandoned me because they felt I'd brought them shame. And then there was the continual deterioration of my body, and all the suffering. You want to tell me what all of this is supposed to mean?

"It's the means by which you chose to evolve, though you presently don't understand that. To see, or not see, the light depends solely on your will."

If this is true, why are we not told this before we die? Instead we're told about heaven, and hell, and purgatory, depending on the seriousness of your sins. Mine were considered the worst, yet I don't see any demons, and there's no hell, unless it's where I am now.

"The only sin is a lack of love, and even then we can learn from our mistakes. The only hell we create in our minds when we reject the light. Open your heart, and trust that just by wanting the light, you will see it."

When this angry soul was finally willing to see the light, he said:

I would never have believed this.... If I had to go through all that suffering to get here, it was well worth it.... Thank you for helping me discover this magnificent light.

The following message from our teachers further clarifies the topic of illness:

Our bodies function according to our way of thinking, within the boundaries of what our higher self has set out to do. When we begin earthly life, we forget our learning objectives. If we intend to learn humility yet do nothing except waste the opportunities that arise, our higher self will create other situations to stimulate the development of that virtue. It isn't a case of a cruel destiny, but of wisdom because the purpose of earthly life is to improve ourselves, not just to have a good time.

If we could live with perfect acceptance, we would be happy because true happiness comes from not opposing what life sets before us, but in acting in accordance with the law of love.

When we say the body's condition depends on how we think, we mean that if our thinking is negative, the energy blockages in the astral body will find expression in the physical body, resulting in deterioration or disease. When our thoughts are positive, the result is a balancing energy that prevents this.

Of course, there are people who are very egocentric yet have no diseases or deformities. This is because their higher self has chosen to have a healthy lifetime in order to discover balance. If they fail to overcome their negativity, the resultant toxins will be expelled by means of a serious disease in a future lifetime.

Conversely, there are many spiritually advanced people with very serious health problems. This corresponds to the higher self's desire to elevate itself and bring its cycle of incarnations to an end, once and for all.

The decision to experience sacrifice in physical life serves to move us forward in our detachment from physicality. Suffering is not required for opening our consciousness, but it can be a very effective method.

The soul may enjoy expressing itself in physical matter and so may seek pleasant experiences that are of very little use in an evolutionary sense. But a time comes when the soul feels compelled to move forward toward the light that is its Source. This impulse is always within us and, ultimately, it steps forward to lead us to our destiny.

If someone experiences an illness that cannot be cured due to financial limitations, it's because the higher self chose to be purified in this way, not because of universal cruelty. Sometimes a solution to a specific illness or difficulty comes to us. But if no solution is available, we are to learn acceptance. To struggle desperately against our situation cannot result in a positive outcome.

We must adapt to our limitations, which are designed so that we may learn. Trying to force the issue only leads to more misfortune. Always wishing for what you don't have, constitutes attachment to the material world. This is why the higher self designs lessons in detachment and acceptance meant to help us let go of the physical plane.

Pain is nothing more than the result of unfulfilled desires, and it worsens when we don't know how to let go of the objects of our attachment, whether loved ones, or possessions, or our social standing. We must let go *of everything because each person experiences exactly what he or she was meant to, and we cannot change our destiny.*

6

Unexpected Death

~

The wise man does not hoard.
The more he allows for others,
The more he benefits himself.
The more he gives to others,
The more he gets himself.
The way of heaven does one good
But never does one harm.
The way of the wise man is to act
But not to compete.
~ Tao Te Ching

The exact moment of death is not always predetermined. Throughout our lives on the physical plane, we are presented with different options, always with the objective of assisting in our evolution. If we choose a learning path then forget what we had intended to accomplish, we require a new stimulus to help us achieve those goals.

Our physical experience comes to an end when our learning objective is concluded. If our life takes a wrong turn, however, the consequences may lead to premature termination of our experience on earth. This occurs with the full agreement of our higher self, which would rather bring the experience to a prompt conclusion than continue to accumulate negativity. This is the case in many premature deaths, be they by accident or homicide. The latter is more frequent, actually, as it is one means of discharging some of the karma generated by a distorted attitude.

Death by Homicide

One example of the circumstance we have just mentioned is that of a young man who was kidnapped and, after several days, murdered. The pain caused to those around him helped with the spiritual development of those who were able to overcome the ordeal. At the time of the young man's death, Carmen received the following message:

His mother is reaching out to our plane and asking for help, and we will assist her in accepting this difficult event. Help her understand that her son's sacrifice was necessary to comply with his higher self, which did not want to continue being entangled in a life that wasn't helping achieve spiritual progress. She must understand that what happened is the best thing for his soul.

The following is the testament of a soul who experienced premature death by murder:

I always followed the decrees of religion very closely, but the reason was fear of taking responsibility for myself. Deep down, I knew that I should look for something deeper and more truthful, as I had the openness and intelligence to do so. But I also knew that this would compel me to change my behavior. Religion was a shield behind which I could hide since, by following its precepts—in other words, by repenting and confessing— all is forgiven. I didn't delve deeper into the importance of loving acts, and the purgatory and hell that correspond to cause and effect. I was content to interpret religion as it suited me, and I thought that my knowledge was enough to put me on the right side of religion.

Despite my gifts, I lived a selfish and completely unproductive life. I was very gifted in that life, because I had decided before coming to become a spiritual leader. But out of laziness, I didn't go through with it. This failure tainted my whole life. I followed only my primitive urges and allowed myself to be carried away by basic instincts. I can't say that I was completely negative; I was a very good friend and didn't deliberately harm anyone. But gradually my life began to deteriorate. I numbed my mind with alcohol to escape a reality, created by myself, that was largely negative.

That's when my higher self decided to put a stop to a course of events worsening by the day. Murder was chosen as the means to rattle me and bring me back to spiritual reality. And so it was. It was very painful to go in that way since, despite my failures, I was very attached to life. It was difficult for me to let go for two reasons: one, fear of the punishment I believed I deserved; and two, attachment to the things that made me feel important and highly intelligent. I should tell you that intelligence and dullness are qualities we choose before incarnating in order to complete a specific learning task. Where I am now, what's important is having a consciousness that is more or less open.

However difficult, my death was very instructive because the remorse it generated has helped me understand everything that we should not do. We learn from our wise decisions, and we learn even more from our mistakes.

Although death by murder is not always due to karma, it generally results from a similar act carried out in a previous experience. We cleanse our karma by receiving what we previously gave, and our pain neutralizes the harm we caused in the past.

Experiencing murder is painful because life comes to an abrupt and unexpected end. But this is sometimes necessary to neutralize the negativity of having murdered a fellow human in the past. Once this is understood and accepted, the karma disappears, and the soul is freed of that burden.

Often the soul of a murdered person wanders about in the lower astral plane contemplating revenge. This fixation can last a long time and can even influence several lifetimes. Vengeful souls may go after their prey, following them from one lifetime to another, trying to inflict as much harm as possible. This is part of a murderer's karma, from which he or she can never be freed until that act is neutralized by either pain or love. If a murderer kills again in a subsequent experience, his or her karma is multiplied, and he or she will attract pain and misfortune. Killing is not right, of course, and neither is the taking of life as punishment, as in the case of the death penalty. No one has the right to abort another's life experience.

These days, we see a great deal of pain in the world: serial murders, rapes, kidnappings, and every kind of horror. Our teachers tell us not to despair because we are witnessing the deep cleansing of many compromised souls. And what will happen to those beings who commit such acts of madness? After their current lifetimes, they will go to a place that matches their low vibrational frequency. They will not be allowed to return here with unrepentant attitudes of hatred, so once this generation has passed, those with very low vibrational frequencies will be gone.

We must, however, make it clear that it is not a question of *lex talionis*—an eye for an eye, a tooth for a tooth—but rather that these experiences are instrumental in our personally understanding whatever harm we have caused our fellow man. These are merely lessons, not punishment nor vengeance. In all likelihood, we have all assumed the roles of both victim and perpetrator many times, since the best method for learning a lesson is to live it.

Stealing is Wrong, but I Didn't See it That Way

Fernando, a businessman whom Carmen had known casually, was murdered while leaving his office one day. The rumor was that it might have been a crime of passion involving another man. This is what Fernando told us a few days after his death:

I'm hearing voices telling me to reach out to you because you know how to help people in my situation. Tell me where to go. I have no idea. Someone who envied me took my life. I was beaten to death, not because I was homosexual but as vengeance for an injustice. I've paid for my dishonesty, and now I don't know where to go. I'm in a black hole filled with guilt and the desire for revenge.

Stealing is wrong, but I didn't see it that way. When we're on earth, we justify and forgive ourselves for the wrongs we do. As soon as we lose the physical body, though, everything becomes clear and we realize what we did wrong. I don't know what's waiting for me now, and that terrifies me. Between earthly life and God's judgment, there is only this cold place where there's no one and nothing but regret.

"God doesn't punish," we told Fernando. "God is love."

How can it be that we can do wrong without being punished?

"Inharmonious behavior is merely a part of our learning process so that we may discover the true path. God does not judge; only you are judging. A lovely life is awaiting you."

Your words are comforting, but I'm not sure that I believe you. It's not what I was taught, and I don't think you know more than everyone else. Who do you think you are to predict what will happen in this place if you've never been here?

We explained again that there was nothing to fear and that Fernando just needed to ask to see the light. Fernando continued to doubt.

It's alarming to be communicating with people I hardly know. You are spiritualists, I suppose, so you probably have dealings with the devil.

"We're only here to help. What's keeping you in that place of darkness is your own guilt and self-judgment. You only have to open yourself to love, accepting with humility what your life was and what your reality is now. Place yourself in God's hands. Ask to be taken to Him."

Seeing my selfishness so clearly is terrifying. Heaven is for the pure and hell for those who act wrongly. I don't know which I deserve.

It took us a while to calm Fernando down because his guilt was enormous, and he couldn't see beyond it. We never stopped concentrating on sending him love, and gradually he began to see the light. Like so many others, once he was moving toward the light, Fernando was overcome by feelings of love and acceptance.

In this case, as in many others, there were voices urging a soul to approach us. Beings on "the other side" sometimes cannot communicate with the recently deceased, whose attention is still focused on this plane. Because those souls are still vibrating very near earthly frequency, they can more easily hear us, which is why we're often asked to intervene.

Death by Suicide

Death by suicide is the refusal to carry on with a plan for dissolving karma during a particular lifetime. This refusal ultimately results in more pain because, once you've arrived in the afterlife, you realize that you interrupted an important process. What you were trying to escape still exists, but with another focus. Now you experience regret for not having had the courage to follow the plan to the end.

Suicide sometimes occurs in cases of severe depression or insanity. These conditions are considered illnesses, and they are, but they are also means of escaping reality. As previously stated, illness originates in the astral body as an emotional imbalance. The resulting physical malfunction may lead to altered brain chemistry, and so chronic depression or insanity. It's true that there are people with a genetic predisposition to such illnesses, but ultimately, we choose these situations in order to transcend them. If we live in harmony, mental illnesses do not take over, but if we allow ourselves to be carried away by the demands of the ego, the consequence will be an imbalance that may manifest as depression or dementia.

After a case of suicide, the soul usually sees its act as reprehensible and cowardly, but the soul is not reproached or punished in any way. We should remember that free will is sacred, and the universe always respects our decisions. So the only one who imposes guilt following an act of suicide is the one who committed it.

In many cases, suicides wander aimlessly in the limbo of the lower astral plane, completely lost. Expecting to have put an end to their lives, they find that this is not so. This results in despair because they still feel the same way as before, only worse because it's compounded by remorse. We see this in the following case, which came to our attention during a session of our meditation group:

I lacked balance in my life, and my situation worsened to the point where I was experiencing serious depression. I felt that the best thing for my family was for me to go, so I decided to commit suicide. Unfortunately, I now see that this fixed nothing. The depression I felt while alive still haunts me, but more intensely, as it's compounded by the suffering I inflicted on others. Now I don't know what to do. I feel like a bottomless abyss is swallowing me. Voices tell me to reach out to your group, so I'm trying. I feel waves of warmth and wellbeing coming from you.

As is our custom, we urged this soul to let go of his guilt and seek the light. It took a great deal of persuasion and loving energy, but finally he was able to free himself. This is another example of how guilt entraps and disables us, preventing our accessing the world of spirit. The last communication we received from this soul was:

God is love. How long it has taken for me to understand this!

Many different circumstances can lead us to suicide. The most common, as noted, is the refusal to accept conditions previously agreed upon. It comes down to refusing to suffer, which we later view as cowardice. Other people may put an end to their lives to minimize a scandal, thus not staining the name of our families.

Suicide for political or religious reason occurs when a person refuses to accept new political or moral ideas he or she feels are wrong, and believes that his or her self-sacrifice will set an example. When an individual cuts short his or her life for reasons of altruism, in effect helping others, it is not a case of cowardice. It's a heroic suicide, when someone gives his or her life to save others. Such variables can mitigate the sense of guilt that accompanies suicide, but it's important to know that every life experience is a precious opportunity for spiritual advancement. To waste such an opportunity is always cause for regret.

We should clarify that, to the Creator, no act is reprehensible. There are only acts that bring us closer to, or place us farther from, Himself. When our decisions are contrary to universal harmony, cosmic law will see to it that we return to the right path. For each of us, good and bad are woven into the experiences of our lives in such a way that we ultimately return to our Source.

I Wasted Half my Opportunities

Bianca, one of my students, arrived one day for group meditation with a letter in her hand.

"Carmen, this letter," she said, "is from a friend I haven't heard from in a long time. I'd like you to read it and tell me what you think. I don't know why, but I feel that it's a letter of goodbye."

Bianca, an Italian, had attended school in Switzerland with an English girl named Elizabeth. Theirs was one of those rich adolescent friendships that promised to last a lifetime. Then, at age twenty, Elizabeth was in a skiing accident that left her paralyzed and wheelchair-bound. Of course, Elizabeth's life became extremely difficult, yet she never broke off her friendship with Bianca, who wrote and visited often.

Now twenty years had passed, and Bianca was worried, as she hadn't had a chance to go to England in some time, and her calls were not getting through. Now this letter.

Reluctantly, I accepted the letter and instantly felt a chill run down my spine. My hair even stood on end. Without reading a word, I sensed that the letter signified death. On the surface, it was an innocuous letter, but between the lines was a deep weariness and desperation that was very troubling. I tried to give the letter back to Bianca, but she asked me to keep it and so perhaps receive more information about her friend. I agreed that, should anything come to me, I would let her know.

The following day, I received this message:

Bianca, I send you my most affectionate regards and best wishes for your continuing life. As you have gathered, after everything I suffered in my most recent, and completely voluntary, life, I have moved on. I can tell you now that I was unable to stand all the suffering required for me to neutralize my karma. Our lives in the material world are incredible opportunities to learn, and believe me when I say that we choose our circumstances.

I chose a very difficult life because I had a lot to learn, but I didn't accomplish everything I wanted because I was resentful and rebellious. As soon as I arrived in this wondrous place, I realized that I had left a lot of work undone.

Always live your life searching for truth, and accept your circumstances, which are always for the purpose of opening your consciousness. Our friendship was the beginning of my spiritual life because of the many deep conversations we shared. Your friendship was always a balm throughout my difficulties. Whenever you have difficulties in your own life, accept them as incentive to learn to let go of worldly values and foolish pride.

I can only tell you that here things are much more clear, and so I know that I wasted half my opportunities. It's true that my ordeal was extreme, but the objective was to learn to detach myself from the material world, which I was able to accomplish only by way of defiance and anger. I can't say that my experience was useless, but I definitely didn't take full advantage of it. My advice to you, dear Bianca, is that you accept your difficult experiences and try to learn what they can teach you. Open yourself to your internal light, and you will find harmony and happiness. —Lizotta.

The signature at the end of the message was the affectionate nickname Bianca had used for Elizabeth, which was unknown to me. Later, Bianca learned that Elizabeth had indeed taken her own life by ingesting an overdose of narcotics.

A Young Man Worried About His Looks

The following message came to us in response to a grieving couple whose young son had committed suicide:

Here I am. Where else would I be but with my parents? I love them so dearly, and I've made them suffer so terribly. I ask their forgiveness for the foolishness I committed. I don't know how I arrived at such a pass just because of a love affair that didn't work out.

Yes, I was guilty of spitefulness; and yes, I had a hang-up about my looks, which I blamed for my lack of success, both at work and in matters of love. I'm so, so sorry for what I did. It was very foolish, and nothing can be done about it now.

When I looked upon my lifeless body, I was overwhelmed with despair because I realized at once what a stupid thing I had done. Since then, I've been looking for a way to tell my parents how very much I love them and that I'm sorry for what I did. Thank you, whomever you are, for giving me this opportunity to speak to them.

"Don't worry," we answered. "A marvelous life is waiting for you. Punishment does not exist. God is love and so does not judge."

You say such wonderful things, but they are hard for me to believe. How can a happy life be waiting for me after what I did? No one ever told me such a thing before. I've always heard that there's no forgiveness for suicide.

"God's mercy is infinite."

The expectation of God's mercy is very comforting. So is my parents' forgiveness.

This soul finally called for the light, after which he said the following:

Heaven is opening its doors. It's true. A marvelous, loving light is pulling me inexorably toward it. I am enveloped by infinite love, happiness, and forgiveness. How fantastic! I'm encountering the actual heaven. I didn't know this existed. Despite what I did, I am being welcomed here with infinite love.

Addressing his parents, he continued:

Don't cry anymore. I'm happy, and as I go further into the light, I begin to better understand what life is about, which is to act with love. I think that's the only thing that's worthwhile. Goodbye, my dearly beloved parents. It's not really goodbye because I know one day we'll see each other again. Meanwhile, I will watch over you from here, giving you the strength to go on. Rest assured that your son is happy and that this experience will help you to seek God all the more.

Many different issues lead people to suicide. For some, it's because they have everything; for others, it's because they don't have what they most desire; still others are tempted to suicide because of their attachment to what has been taken away from them. But we all have the opportunity to learn from our difficulties, rather than succumb to negativity.

I Never Had to Make an Effort to Succeed

I shot myself because I was an idiot. I was angry at life, so I drank to escape reality. Why, you might ask, was I unhappy when I had everything. True, from a financial point of view, I lacked for nothing, yet I didn't know the meaning of my existence. People sought me out for what I had, not for who I was. I never had to make an effort to succeed, and that can leave a person feeling maddeningly empty. If you never make an effort, you have nothing to look forward to. My life was lonely and meaningless. Only my mother loved me for who I was, but she, too, was immersed in that same emptiness where wishes are granted far too easily.

I was out drinking that night, and when I left that last place, I felt absolute despair and rage. I pulled out my gun, wanting to kill someone—the whole world—but I found nothing better to put a bullet through than myself.

Now here I am where no one can see or hear me, and without a clue as to what to do next. This place is even worse than what I experienced on earth. There's no one to talk to, and I'm alone with my regret at lacking the courage to go on living.

We helped this soul to free him from guilt and find the light. One of the last things he said was:

In this light, I feel love, forgiveness and acceptance, all of which I wanted to feel in my life. Dear friends, don't do what I did. Live what you are meant to live, with love, because what awaits you afterward is incredible.

I Couldn't Bear my Loneliness

This is the case of a man who, after the death of his wife, couldn't deal with being alone:

I committed suicide because I couldn't bear my loneliness. I was inextricably attached to my wife, and once she was gone, I sank into despair. I took my life hoping to find her, but I have only found darkness and cold, in addition to a great deal of guilt. I didn't think about the hurt I would cause my family by this act. Now I'm tormented by regret. I was always selfish, only interested in my own wellbeing, which was supported by my wife's total devotion. Now I see all the harm I caused by my egocentric behavior. I don't feel that I deserve my children's forgiveness, but more than anything else, that's what I wish for.

As is our custom, we counseled this unhappy soul and persuaded him to ask for the light.

The following text on suicide comes from our teachers:

Suicide is nothing more than an individual's decision to not go on with the current third-dimensional life experience. This act does not entail any punishment, just as no human act elicits punishment, but there is regret for not having had the courage to complete the experience, plus surprise that life continues when you thought you had ended it.

What you had previously resolved to do in that lifetime is merely postponed until the next experience. While there is no punishment, per se, there are effects. When you cut short a life experience, the same lesson will come up in a future life, only it may be more challenging the next time around.

In some cases, suicide is incipient in a person's character, corresponding to an unconscious rejection of the world of matter. There are souls who decide to go to earth but, once there, lack the courage to deal with all the obstacles. So begins an unconscious desire to end the experience. Even an unconscious choice is a choice, and souls who reject physical life in this way may repeat the same behavior many times, as the memory is stored in the emotional body. This method of escape can become a habit.

Madness is another escape from physical reality. Although insanity seems to be an acquired or genetic illness, it is a pre-birth decision like all the others. To be born with that tendency is an opportunity for growth, as it presents huge obstacles. But once the illness manifests, it becomes a convenient method of escaping those same obstacles.

Accidental Death

Accidental death is not really accidental. Whether death is caused by the crash of an automobile or airplane, or by drowning, or by some other seemingly random cause, the event was staged to open the consciousness of those remaining behind. Souls choose to die this way in order to provoke pain that leads loved ones to see beyond their attachments. Those who die in an accident have an opportunity, as well, as the pain of abruptly leaving the world helps them understand that this life is not the true one. These experiences serve to coax souls away from the clamorous attractions of earth. Especially poignant are cases of children dying suddenly. Generally, such souls agree to come down for a short time out of love for those whose spiritual growth will be aided by means of the drama.

Pain, as we have already seen, is a purifying energy always possible to bear because, when it becomes intolerable, we lose consciousness. As for non-physical pains such as depression or grief, these always motivate us to seek refuge in the world of spirit. To see our moments of pain as impulses toward God, is to see with true clarity.

Our guides tell us that, when a soul leaves the body following an accident, there is a lot of disorientation because there was no opportunity to prepare. In such cases, our prayers are important. Those "on the other side" help, too, but in many cases it isn't enough. Those who remain in the world should pray to help the departed let go of the world, or their astonishment and anger may keep them stuck for a long time.

I Fell Asleep While Driving, and Now I Find Myself in a Dark Place

It is common for people to think of themselves as righteous, or even saintly, when in fact their behavior is largely contrary to love. After death, these people wrestle with their pride. They may have expectations of heaven opening up to welcome them with a huge celebration. When they see this is not the case, these souls tend to become indignant and retreat even farther into their pride. The alternative is to accept that we were mistaken and use our despair to move us to ask for help, which is immediately supplied.

To wit:

> *I'm told that you can help me. I don't know what's*
> *happened to me. I fell asleep while driving, and now I*
> *find myself in a dark place. If this is death, it's horrible.*
> *I don't understand. I was always devoutly religious, so*
> *I expected to find a purgatory for sinners and a heaven*
> *for the pure. I don't know what I could have done wrong,*
> *or even whether this is purgatory. The important thing*
> *is, how do I get out of here?*

This request came from the soul of a woman who had just
perished in a car accident. As always, we spoke to her of the
non-existence of divine punishment and the need for her to
accept her present circumstances.

> *You say that God doesn't punish. Then why did he make*
> *me suffer so much in life? I never understood it, and I*
> *certainly didn't accept it, any more than I accept being*
> *here now. I don't believe a word of it. You are certainly*
> *witches for saying that God doesn't punish, and for*
> *calling my attitude arrogant. I don't want to listen to*
> *you anymore. I'll just figure out something on my own.*

A week later, we were again contacted by this soul, whom
our teachers characterized as "very rebellious." What she
encountered on the astral plane did not correspond to her
expectations, and she could find no comfort because she didn't
believe what she was being told, nor could she accept being
"shut out" of heaven. She insisted that she had always practiced
what the church taught.

We replied: "If you feel shut out, it's due to your way of
thinking. What the church preaches above all is love and
humility, and that is where we human beings fail. It's difficult for
us to forgive those we believe have harmed us, and it's difficult
for us to be generous, as we always want to be the center of

attention. We all want to be recognized for what we do, and we all try to control those around us. These attitudes are lacking in love, and they alienate us from others.

"God does not punish. Painful lives, such as the one you just experienced, are not punishments but are designed so that we may learn to forgive, to stop coveting control, and to be more humble. God is absolute goodness, and He waits with infinite patience for us to become aware of our errors. Your life was a tool for learning. The only thing that remains for you to do is to open yourself up, with humility, to the light that awaits your desire to see it."

What a load of rubbish! I don't understand how, if all that is true, it's not spoken of in church. I do sense some element of truth in what you say because it brings me peace, and that must mean something. But how can I get out of here when I don't see any description of light?

"You'll be able to see the light as soon as you put aside your defiance at not having found what you expected. Just ask for it with humility, and with the faith that everything that happens is for our highest good, though we may not immediately understand it. If you can do that, you will begin to see a radiance that emanates from the world of spirit, which is the light of the Creator. There you will find peace, love, and resolution. It's only your pride that keeps you from seeing it."

I hadn't understood the meaning of humility before now. It's faith that you speak of. But I still don't understand something. If we do everything that religion commands, how can it still turn out that we are in the wrong?

"Perhaps you were concerned with appearances, with observing the precepts in terms of external behaviors. That was not Christ's message. All that really counts according to Jesus is acting from love. This means accepting others unconditionally, forgiving rather than judging, and not placing ourselves above anyone. We all have the same amount of light; we only differ in how much light we allow to manifest, and that depends on not letting ourselves be carried away by the arrogant ego."

What you say is new to me. Yet, at the same time, I seem to remember it, as though something inside me is bringing it back to mind. I'm feeling a warm energy coming from you, and it's helping my consciousness become clearer. I now see that I haven't always acted from love, and that I've used religion as a shield.

*But my real stumbling stone has been pride. I didn't understand my husband, and I didn't know how to forgive him, so I was always full of resentment toward him, and toward life. Now I'm seeing a radiance that's growing brighter and brighter. It's a wonderful light. You really can't imagine.... From it emanates infinite peace and love. I'm going toward it. It's pulling me.... Thank you.... I'm told that you're writing a book about cases such as mine. You must make this most emphatically clear to your readers: **if we don't understand what love is, we're missing the meaning of life.***

Sudden Death

An unexpected death is not always a negative. Depending on the individual's evolutionary state, this kind of death can be a blessing. Although the soul has to let go of the body quite abruptly and there is no time for gradual detachment, needless pain and suffering may be avoided.

Generally speaking, we can say that the illness that ends in death is the preparatory process for that death. Little by little, the higher bodies let go of the physical body, thus facilitating the process of emotional detachment. This doesn't necessarily mean that detachment is problematic in cases of sudden death, but it can certainly be confusing.

Our deepest reality is the desire to return to God. While on earth, we may forget about our Source, but deep inside there is always a desire for something indescribable yet compelling. There's a great emptiness that cannot be filled by anything material—neither power, nor money, nor human love. There is a universal attraction of souls toward an indefinable something higher than themselves. What humans seek throughout their many existences is union with the Whole, as do all forms of creation, which can but respond to the call of their Creator.

Those immersed in their own pride, which blocks the call of their Source, eventually realize that there is something more meaningful than their own conceit. This occurs when they find no satisfaction in anything else they try.

When, at the moment of death, human beings feel that hunger for the infinite, the natural response is to cry out for God. The immediate response is a warm, welcoming light overflowing with love and peace. The cases described in this book are the exceptions, souls who for the reasons detailed, do not immediately go toward the light. But love and divine mercy are always available to welcome those who are open.

Next is the story of a woman who died suddenly of a heart attack. Her daughter, worried that she might be disoriented in the afterlife, asked us to send her light. The deceased was someone who had led a normal life, not particularly inclined toward spirituality yet basically good.

This soul was allowed to speak to us, and this is what she said:

I left without warning, and now I'm in the place from which there is no return. My beloved daughter, from here I can see your concern for me, but don't worry. I'm fine. There's a wondrous light where I am, and incredibly I can communicate with you. I don't know how. When I arrived here, I was welcomed by many loved ones whom I thought I had lost forever. Though we're told on earth that death doesn't exist, while we're on earth we can't be absolutely sure.

I didn't suffer at all. When I woke up, I realized I was no longer in the world but in a different place that I didn't understand very well. I reached out to divine mercy, asking for help and forgiveness for my faults, and right away an indescribable light opened up. It was so full of love. The feeling was indescribable. People I knew came out to meet me, smiling and brimming with love. I can tell you that the punishment of purgatory does not exist. There is only the immense love of the Creator.

I saw my whole life with alarming clarity, including all the right and wrong things I had done; and I understood that the only really worthwhile thing is to act without egotism. This can't be understood in all its magnitude while we're on earth, despite what religion tells us, but here you understand everything with astonishing clarity. I can tell you that here we have regrets that cause us pain, but the beings of light who help us review our lives, give us such intense love that all guilt is washed away. Tell everyone that the only thing worthwhile in life is love, not selfishness, and that love is the true mission and meaning of life.

Cases such as the above are most common, given that most humans, when we meet death, intuitively cry out for divine mercy, and that's all that's required for us to see the light.

The idea that only acting from love is worthwhile in life, is a constant in the messages from those who have experienced death. As soon as the light envelops them, they are given this understanding. Following is one more case in point, that of a man who died suddenly and whose initial reaction was anger at having lost the life he so loved. After going toward the light and receiving its message, he reported as follows:

It's incredible, but a luminous crack has opened before me, emitting a light. As I go toward the light, it grows larger. I keep going along this sort of black tunnel at whose end a light is growing brighter and brighter.

It's amazing! I can't fathom why we're not told about this while we're in the world. Everyone should know that this is heaven. There's such a warm feeling of love, and peace, and happiness, that it's unimaginable while you're in the world. Now I understand why they say God is love. It's true!

*Now I see, emerging from that irresistible light, beings coming toward me with outstretched arms, helping me leave my shadows.... Thank you, thank you, a thousand times over, for your help. But tell everyone! Tell all those who, like me until now, don't understand what life is really about! I realize now that the only thing with any value is love, and all the rest is garbage. I don't understand why this is not better explained, this whole process of living and the non-existence of death. This passage into true life is difficult only when we're not adequately prepared. We're told about love, but only in the context of a lot of nonsense like hell and divine punishment. Our God is **love,** and the idiocies we perpetrate are paid for only with remorse once our minds become clear in this wondrous light.*

*I'm told you're writing a book. Then say this, and say this loud and clear: **death does not exist!** It's only a shift from an unreal state to a real one. In this place everything becomes clear, and we realize that the only things that matter are our acts of love toward others: of giving without expecting to receive in return, and of forgiving those we feel offended by.... I'm going now, moving toward eternal happiness, my heart bursting with the love I knew only sporadically during my time on earth.*

We have described some cases of sudden or violent death, but many more deaths occur naturally, when the purpose established by the soul has been satisfied. If the soul has chosen beforehand to experience a slow, painful death, so it will be until the soul decides that the lesson has been learned.

There are other times when our attachment to the physical world lengthens the dying process unnecessarily. In these cases, our higher self, which knows that remaining in the world is no longer necessary or helpful, comes into conflict with our lower self, which wishes to continue with physical existence at all cost. Eventually, of course, the lower self acquiesces.

7

Mediums, Altered States of Consciousness, and Sorcery

~

Is it life, or is it death?
Death is but life falling into the night,
For from the night, morning emerges.
Only when day, night, and life become one,
And are absorbed into that from whence they came,
Shall you have redemption and unite with God
And your fellow beings.
~ Paul Twitchell

Everything that exists is a manifestation of God. Together the Creator and his creation form a unity, a single body within which we exist, connected quite naturally to the entire universe. The moment, however, we feel ourselves to be limited and separate from our surroundings, we lose the ability to communicate with the cosmos. Suddenly, gone are such natural abilities as mediumship, channeling, telepathy, and extrasensory perception. Though we never really lose these

163

abilities, egocentricity and excessive rationality do obscure them in our awareness. Yet this power is slumbering in every human being and is awakened to a greater or lesser extent.

Mediumship, or psychism, is simply the practice of entering into contact with other realities. It's the ability to perceive events and circumstances outside the realm of time and space, as well as to receive messages from other beings, whether on the physical plane or elsewhere. These abilities do not require the use of our physical senses. Telepathy, premonition, and intuition are examples of this kind of awareness. In the first case, we perceive another person's thoughts without need of words or consideration of distance. In the second case, we are aware beforehand of an event that takes place in the future. As for intuition, it comes from our ever-present connection to the higher self.

Dimensions that vibrate at different frequencies overlap each other, in effect occupying the same space. Thus, dimensions should not be thought of as separate. Because they interpenetrate, beings in different dimensions can communicate by tuning in to other vibrational frequencies. Whether incarnate beings raise their frequency or disincarnate beings lower theirs, contact is established by means of intention. Humans with a greater aptitude for communicating with other realities are known as sensitives, psychics, mediums or channelers.

The word *medium* just means intermediary, so we are all mediums to a greater or lesser extent. We all act as intermediaries among the various dimensions to the extent that we open ourselves to their vibration. Actually, without being aware of it, we are continuously receiving messages from multiple dimensions, or planes. As said before, the guides who help us open our awareness communicate telepathically with their protégés, though not always as successfully as they would like. It should be noted that the frequency at which the psychic is vibrating at the moment he or she makes contact, determines the level at which contact will be made. With regard to this, we are told the following:

The channeler must be cleansed of the influence of the ego, and must be constantly alert for its appearance. Channelers accomplish this through discernment and self-observation. If we want a very high entity such as Jesus or Mary to communicate through us, our vibrations must be at a very high frequency, but very valid messages also come from less exalted sources. Actually, if a communication appears to be from the very highest of entities, it's most likely a test to gauge the discernment (and the ego) of the channeler. This is not trickery but a necessary testing procedure.

From whom the information comes is less important than what the message says. Be wary of information tinged with fanaticism. Such messages are another means of testing channelers, and their followers, as well. Discernment must always be practiced, accepting only what is positive and useful. It is wrong to never question what is received through channeling. As has already been said, the work of expanding consciousness is a matter of personal effort, and it always involves discernment. The truth will not show itself unless you make an effort to meet it halfway.

The work of discernment is aided by our soul's integration with its entirety. When the message seems to come from inside you, it's the higher self helping us discern what is of value and what is not.

Mankind's current state of evolution makes difficult (sic) our experience of the light dwelling within each of us. For this reason, humans need guides to act as intermediaries between the very high truths, which vibrate rapidly, and our own humble nervous systems. It is we, your disembodied brothers and sisters who remain very near your vibration, who attempt to clarify these higher truths. Now that we have left our bodies, it's easier for us to understand many things, as we have been lovingly taught by others higher on the vibrational scale.

> *We dwell on various levels governed by our own vibrational frequencies. Those beings dwelling on higher levels are able to descend to our level, but we cannot reach theirs. However, there is continual communication throughout the whole cosmos; it's like an enormous, interactive communications network. You can't imagine the intelligence and wisdom with which everything has been designed. Every act by every human has repercussions and so calls forward a universal response aimed at restoring the harmony disturbed by a given act.*

A common example of psychic abilities is our perception of positive or negative feelings coming from other people. These are energy vibrations that we pick up without need of the senses.

Basically, mediumship or psychism comes down to being in touch with the universe. Were we fully open, we would be in constant communication with mountains, plants, animals, and so forth. There are different forms of sensitivity, such as clairvoyance, which enables us to see, without the physical eyes, events from the past, present and future; clairaudience is the ability to hear voices, music or messages, without the use of our ears; there are also various trance states during which automatic speaking or writing can occur. Automatic writing is a medium in a trance state lending his or her pen to an unseen entity. During the process, there is no personal awareness of what is being written; in intuitive writing, the medium is awake and writes down what is telepathically received, without prior knowledge of the words or ideas that emerge.

A trance is an extraordinary state of consciousness during which our sense of ego identity temporarily diminishes or vanishes. During these moments, it's possible to receive or transmit information from other dimensions. The trance may be light or deep. Light trances or self-hypnotic states are those under which automatisms occur without loss of consciousness. In deep trances, the medium is taken over by a spirit who controls the entire process. In some instances, we can witness changes in the medium's voice or gestures as the entity takes over.

There are mediums who do healing work, serving as channels between universal energy and individuals whose energy is out of balance, resulting in illness. Some such mediums even perform psychic surgery, channeling light entities who work on the astral plane and make use of mediums in the same way a medical surgeon would use a knife to remove a tumor. This is what our teachers have to say on the subject:

Healing takes place in the astral body, which, as the energy mold of the physical body, is where illness originates. To clarify: if a surgical procedure takes place, the psychic standing before the physical body does nothing more than remove what has already been removed in the astral body. If, for instance, a bone replacement is carried out, that operation has already taken place at the astral level, and the bone implanted in the physical body will knit according to what was done in the astral body. How can one penetrate the physical body without cutting it open and leaving a scar? A cavity is opened in the astral body, in response to the intention of the entities working on that plane, and the physical body follows suit. The medium working on the three-dimensional plane merely follows instructions, that is, serves as an instrument.

Other psychic healers work in different ways, sometimes using the power of their own minds. An illness can be taken out of a patient's body, for instance, by way of dematerialization. The illness, or diseased tissue, may then materialize outside the physical body. This work, too, requires assistance from more elevated entities working on the astral level.

We should seek knowledge of universal law in order to return home and help those who come after us to rise on the evolutionary scale. This knowledge is based on personal effort to work internally to expand our consciousness toward unity.

Of course, many people want to skip steps and access higher knowledge or expanded states through certain exercises and breathing techniques that release the energy of the chakras. In these cases, one's experiences do not correspond to his or her spiritual development. For this reason, we may have experiences we are unable to handle. Similarly, by ingesting drugs that alter our state of consciousness, we may be able to perceive realities that, under normal conditions, would not be accessible. But to artificially project ourselves into other realities is hazardous, as we may be overwhelmed by our own internal imbalances and projections. The danger lies in not being at the correct vibrational level for these trips to other planes. Unable to navigate precisely, we may wind up partially or completely stuck in the dimensions where we find ourselves.

Altered states of consciousness can be defined as those in which individuals free themselves from limitations associated with consensus reality. In such states, the boundaries between self and environment become blurred.

If our desire is to come into contact with the spiritual plane while still living in the physical one, we need to raise our rate of vibration by breaking down our sense of separation, meaning the ego. After, we can return to the vibration of the physical plane by once more lowering our vibrational frequency. When we travel to other planes by artificial means, such as drugs, there is always the danger that we may be unable to come back because the trip was accomplished without the required vibrational acceleration. Hence, ecstatic states and mystical experiences are best accomplished through spiritual work that raises our vibrations, thus expanding our consciousness.

Sorcerers and Sorcery

In a literal sense, thinking is creative. Our minds have the power to give form and substance to whatever we concentrate on. While unknown to most people, there are laws and forces in the universe very well known to certain individuals who use them either for or against other people. We all have unimaginable power, and we can use it to move certain energies, to obtain certain abilities, and to create elementals.

Elementals are defined as, among other things, vibrational beings created by our will. Our thoughts create these entities, whose vibrational state corresponds to that of their creator, to whom they are bound, and whom they serve. Elementals are frequently used by sorcerers for black magic and who, together with the evil entities they call for help, serve them in the practice of what is called "witchcraft."

Elementals also exist in nature. They can be seen by some sensitives, and such sightings have given rise to stories about gnomes, fairies, goblins, elves, and so forth. These beings, while not incarnate, do live on earth, and have a developing consciousness. Just like all the rest of creation, elementals are in the process of evolution back to their Source. They absorb all of humanity's emanations, good and bad, so a loving environment will give rise to loving, benevolent elementals. In the opposite case, malevolent elementals will come to be, filled with envy and negativity. When malevolent elementals come upon an individual seeking the light, they will devote themselves to causing as much trouble as possible, exploiting any crack or flaw in that person's aura for their destructive ends. Such cracks are common, given that humans, though we may be well-intentioned, don't always maintain a uniformly high vibration.

Although elementals are used by sorcerers practicing black magic, these same entities can be used for the common good, such as for cleansing the aura, and physical or emotional healing. This is what is referred to as white magic. When we use these forces for selfish ends or against others, it's considered black magic.

Those to seek new knowledge in order to obtain power succeed. But they can become trapped by that power if they do not use it to achieve union with the Whole, but rather to feel superior to others. Some sorcerers use the power of the mind to escape the physical plane, creating and inhabiting other planes of consciousness where others like them can be found.

Only those instructed in witchcraft are admitted to these planes. The intention of such sorcerers to elevate themselves to the level of the infinite in an exclusive, or selfish way. They have therefore strayed from the true path, which begins with the principle of unity with the Whole where there is no room for exclusion of any kind.

Those beings who seek the power within each of us, but forget that we are all one creature, and forget that knowledge without love is pointless, live in a hell of their own making.

Many so-called sorcerers attain extremely advanced knowledge about the power of the mind, and other realities, and the transmutation of matter—yet they lack love. In fact, they intentionally exclude it from their practices in order to obtain more controlled results.

Black magic begins with intentional withdrawal from the collective consciousness of mankind, as that consciousness influences thoughts and thus actions. Black magicians also break with prevailing human relationship patterns such as love, friendship, and family. Instead, they choose heartlessness. They establish no emotional connections but only use human relationships to their own advantage. Such sorcerers may instruct apprentices in their arts, but it is not for the apprentice's benefit, but to strengthen the planes of power they themselves have created.

Black magicians can become extremely powerful and can even exert control over whomever they choose. But they are not satisfied with the power they can wield in the physical world, which is less and less interesting to them. They increasingly focus on the power they wield in the realities they themselves create, into which they can project themselves.

This "occult" knowledge is really nothing more than using powers of the mind that we all have. Sorcerers are simply more intentional than most of us and apply themselves to a very rigid disciplinary method that goes back to ancient times. In those days there were men who could transcend the physical plane with methods based on love and unity. There were, however, some individuals who sought power over others, and they became sorcerers in the negative sense. Many such people exist today.

This does not mean that acting from love keeps us from progressing in the knowledge of our power, only that the process will take longer. First, we must be able to act in perfect accord with the harmony of the consciousness of the Whole, after which the limitations imposed on us as a consequence of our consciousness of separation are gradually relaxed. These limitations were generated in precise correlation to the power of our mind that thinks and believes itself to be separate from the rest of the cosmos.

Sorcerers use that same mental power to overcome limitations but without eliminating their cause, which is separatism. They favor the benefit of the few by creating planes of consciousness into which a select group may enter. The problem is, those souls remain trapped there until they become aware of the importance of their union with the Whole. Then they usually discover that it's difficult to escape from those realms because they short-circuited the evolutionary process by skipping extremely important steps. Likewise, until we attain true knowledge through love, we will be unable to transcend this three-dimensional plane. We may accomplish reaching the planes created by the minds of sorcerers, but there we'll only find cold and desolation. Their foolishness puts them there, and pride keeps them there.

Once during our weekly meditation group, we received the following message from several beings trapped in a self-made realm:

Our problem is, we can't get out of this place. We created it through many minds acting together to forge a plane of power. We followed techniques designed to awaken the powers of perception and of mind, and those of us who sought power and superiority over others, wound up caught here. Our mistake was forgetting that we are part of a Whole, so any plane that's for only a few, is necessarily limiting.

So here we are, with our very high state of consciousness yet undone by our pride. We ask for your love and prayers to help us leave here. That loving energy, which we ourselves were lacking in our desire to become supermen, gradually breaks down the shell of selfishness and pride that's imprisoning us.

Please continue sending light to those of us trapped here. Your support really does help. We are many, and more arrive each day.

Trapped in a Demonic World

Once during a session of our meditation group, Carmen received a heartbreaking message from a soul requesting the help of the group. To our great surprise, the request came from a friend of ours, Julieta. We had not known about Julieta's passing:

I feel enormous regret and despair because I followed Roberto here so as not to lose him. That desire for control over him made me forget everything I knew. Roberto was looking, not for light, but for power.

I should have known better. Why did I allow myself to be carried away by human love? It's nothing but egotism.

Now, without a great deal of help in the form of love energy, I don't know how I'll ever escape this place. I came here voluntarily. As I've related before, these shamans raise their vibration until they can enter other planes of consciousness created by themselves. They have immense power, and they want more, so they get others, like me, to come here so they can use our energy to sustain their demonic world. I'm trapped here, along with Roberto. He has yet to see the truth of our situation, but I see it clearly, and I now pray to see the light and get out of this place.

Send me light, for it's the only thing that can save me, and He who is omnipotent will forgive my pride. As I've already told you, it's not the first time this has happened to me. I never learn! A rebel to the end.

If our friendship has had any greater purpose, it is this: so that you can help me through this terrible time. I will be so grateful. I can't even bless the Creator from here because the energy is so black and dense that it blocks everything. Bless Him for me, and please help me get out of here. —Julieta

The group concentrated on sending Julieta light and loving energy. One of us visualized her overcoming a great mass of black energy. Afterward, Julieta was seen surrounded by a blue light that elevated her, pulling her out of those dense shadows.

Later we were informed that Julieta was free and undergoing restorative sleep, which is routine for those who have distanced themselves from the light. When she awakens, we were told, her ascension is likely to be rapid, as she is of an advanced consciousness.

Julieta had been a highly educated person with a post-graduate degree in parapsychology from a U.S. university. In her professional life, she had always tried to help others, teaching that the only meaningful path is through love and non-identification with the ego. She was an evolved soul who tried to act in accordance with her beliefs.

Julieta's problem was her deep attachment to her husband, who was a researcher of shamanism from a social and scientific point of view. Roberto's true motivation was a desire to outshine others by discovering knowledge that would uniquely empower him. Julieta, very sincere in her spiritual work, did not share her husband's interest in hoarding power. But her desire to control and change Roberto led her to follow him in his many experiences with shamans, though she knew it wasn't right for her.

They came into contact with people who visited other planes of consciousness through certain practices that bring about a temporary state of bodily death. But playing with fire means getting burned, and Julieta and Roberto lost control during one of their experiences and were unable to return to their bodies.

Julieta had believed herself to be strong enough to resist being dragged into demonic worlds that she could not escape. Her motivation had been to show Roberto that his quest was misguided, as those planes were the creations of sorcerers. Her desire to save Roberto ended up dragging her down with him. We cannot force anyone to change his or her attitude. We must always respect free will, which is something Julieta did not do. Her intentions were good, but she committed error for the sake of a very pathological relationship, which in the end she lost anyway.

One year later, we received the following message from Julieta:

> *I have again been given the opportunity to communicate with you, and I'd like to tell you that it takes a lot of strength to escape the demonic worlds where those sorcerers are! I was able to leave thanks to your invaluable help, and I am now allowed to tell you what those worlds are like.*
>
> *Our thoughts are creative, and by focusing them through exercises and self-discipline, we can accumulate enormous power. For instance, you can dematerialize and materialize objects. You can enter other people's energy fields and take control of their will. You can cause illnesses in people by interfering with their energy supply. All these things are done by sorcerers who practice black*

magic. They also create other planes of consciousness into which they can project themselves in order to enjoy their powers of creation.

But these things are done in the absence of the light of the Whole, so this power is dense and egoic to the point where it becomes very difficult to break away. Let me tell you, those demonic worlds are truly malevolent!

I was very afraid when I found myself there, and I began to feel as cold as ice. The souls there are stupefied by their own power. They can create, as they please, situations that gratify them and demonstrate their power over others. Conflicts don't come up because of strict adherence to hierarchies that reflect the powers of each sorcerer.

I tell you, this is what I now understand to be hell. It hurts me to know Roberto is still there, but that's his decision, and I can't do anything about it. I finally understand that. Everyone there has opportunities to learn, and so eventually to leave, and one day they'll be able to do it. But it's really difficult—extremely so.

My love and gratitude is with all of you. —Julieta

Insofar as doing harm to others through sorcery, a spell succeeds only if the person toward whom it's directed is vibrating in negativity. Witchcraft Cleansing is a means of neutralizing a spell: it uses the same powers of thought but in a positive way. Cleansing is effective because positive energy is always stronger than its counterpart.

A sorcerer who practices black magic must realize that the negative forces he sends out will return to him with even greater intensity. It also returns to the person who commissions the spell, as here, too, the law of cause and effect is always at work. When attacked in this way, the worst response would be to counterattack because this only creates a vicious circle. By keeping our own energy positive, we are immune to such attacks.

Epilogue

~

We conclude with several messages from our teachers that illustrate some of the main ideas this volume has covered:

We reject pain because we don't understand its purpose. Pain raises the vibrations of those who suffer it, be it people or animals. This is because pain opposes our sense of wellbeing in the three-dimensional world. This gives it a positive charge, in the sense that it helps us let go of the attraction of physicality.

We've already said that inharmonious behavior carries a negative charge that needs to be offset for balance to be restored. Since negativity is brought about by a lack of love, the way to reestablish balance is with love. In other words, with a force that opposes the cause of the imbalance. The alternative to love is pain, which too is positive because it carries a charge contrary to our sense of wellbeing and attachment to the material world.

Why must animals endure pain when they are largely unaware of these issues? When an animal suffers, its soul vibration becomes more refined because suffering, in all instances, carries a positive charge, for the reasons previously stated. Animals are, like the rest of creation, in evolution toward the Creator, and their vibration, too, must be elevated. It's not cruelty on the part of The Almighty but a simple law of compensation.

When animals suffer, they don't rebel as humans do. Deep down, they know that pain is not something negative, and they accept it. When pain is accepted, it diminishes to a greater degree than we might think possible because when there is no opposition, pain is markedly reduced and in some instances, disappears.

If only we could understand that everything that happens in the material world has the single objective of helping us evolve and find our way out of this illusory plane. All the pain in the world serves as a driving energy that propels us to the next level of consciousness. There, pain is no longer necessary because we will have understood the meaning of love, which is the reunification of all of creation with their Creator.

The above beautiful passage clarifies the true meaning of pain.

The most unendurable pain is that experienced by individuals who believe that their suffering has no purpose. But those individuals can transform their pain, and their deaths, if they sincerely offer them up for the good and happiness of others. In *The Tibetan Book of the Dead*, the oldest and most important work written on the subject of death, the Tibetan masters recommend a very powerful practice especially apt for those suffering from a terminal illness. It consists of imagining, as intensely as possible, all the people with the same illness and saying very lovingly, "I wish to absorb the suffering of all who have this same illness. I wish them to be free of this affliction, and free from all suffering." The next step is to imagine the illness, tumor, et cetera, leaving their bodies in the form of smoke and entering into your body. When you inhale, you take in all of the suffering, and when you exhale, you imagine your breath issuing as light, healing and wellbeing. Practice this for several minutes, meanwhile believing that others are actually being comforted and healed. This practice gives your death new meaning and can transform your experience. No one need die with the resentment that his or her suffering served no purpose. No suffering is senseless if it is accepted with humility, especially if used to alleviate the suffering of others.

To live in harmony means to live in unity with everything that is. This means accepting the present moment as it comes. We may fight resolutely to improve the conditions of the poor or the unempowered, but we do so without trying to force the results of our struggle. If we sometimes believe that we must accomplish something, but it doesn't work out that way, instead of opposing the outcome, we should let go of our notions about what should be, and accept what is, even if it's not even close to what we'd hoped for.

On no account does this mean that we should not struggle to attain our dreams or reach our goals. At times, life requires fighting through setbacks and opposition. But if life presents an outcome different from the one we had in mind, we must accept it. There must be a reason for it, and maybe later we will come to understand that all was for the best. We must therefore differentiate between fighting to reach a goal and being attached to an outcome. If life opposes our wishes, we will be offered a different solution, and we should accept it.

If we live in the present, neutrally observing all that happens inside of us and outside, as well, we begin to discover that our fixed attitudes keep us from flowing with what is. Every behavior that does not come from love, comes from fear, from a sense of separation, and therefore from the ego, which controls the majority of our acts. The spiritual path is the process of becoming aware of our egotistical attitudes and so, little by little, through self-observation and meditation, dissolving them so that our higher self can manifest. To truly live means to die as a fearful creature with a desire to control everything, and to be reborn as **love,** which is our true essence.

When, in a human life, a soul wastes an opportunity for spiritual growth, all is not lost. That life experience can serve as an example, and maybe that soul won't repeat the same pattern. Once out of the body, the soul can see the harm he or she caused. That helps to shatter negative attitudes, and the soul can go on to the next task filled with humility and willingness. All human beings, no matter their histories, are free to advance toward the light when they wish to do so. There they see their errors clearly, which stimulates them to make corrections. This is the way humans rise toward the spiritual realms.

Many souls find it difficult to leave the lower astral plane. They remain there attached to their desires to experience power and possessions again. Happily, as we have said, the attraction of our origin, our Source, is stronger than any other desire. While it's true that souls can remain in the lower astral for centuries of your time, the prayers of the incarnate, and our own efforts, are ultimately successful.

This is why it's so highly recommended that we pray for the souls "in purgatory." This generates an energy that helps free those souls.

It's really amazing how our Creator has arranged for the development of the consciousness of each and every soul. He gave us free will, and after countless life experiences borne of our will to create, we choose to return to our divine origin. How incredibly generous to share His power with His creatures!

We all began our journey with an undeveloped consciousness, so the law of cause and effect was established to maintain universal order. Then we began experiencing the effects of our creative powers and those powers began to align themselves with universal harmony. But the inharmonious, too, was necessary for the learning process. As we began to understand our choices, we learned about the polar extremes of good and evil. The latter just means making choices that add extra steps to the journey and so intensify our learning. Either way, we eventually arrive at our ultimate destination, the re-discovery of the magnificence of the Creator. If there were no mistakes along the way, we would not be able to fully appreciate our return to Source, nor to understand its meaning. Without having passed through every conceivable shadow, how could we ever say that we know the light?

At the conclusion of our grand journey, we will again experience perfect unity, yet our individuality will continue, as well, and will live forever. Our individual consciousness will be reunified with all others, making it possible for each of us to participate in the experiences of all. We will see how each individual consciousness carried out its specific task, each complementing the other in a grand plan whose purpose was the completion of creation. We will discover true happiness in the balance newly achieved by all that exists. We may never understand the why of creation, but we can and will experience that balance, that deep peace and fulfillment that we sometimes glimpse during meditation when we briefly come into contact with that ocean of which we are one tiny drop.

In the physical world, we live in total confusion, perhaps believing that nothing exists beyond what we perceive with our senses. We expend all our energy trying to stand out, to exert control and so obtain power, to possess material things, and to satisfy sexual desire and the physical senses. Amid all this commotion, we forget what is really important: perfecting the understanding of our own divine nature. We get caught up in details that, at the end of our lives, turn out to be of no use whatsoever.

We must remember that our attachments to family and material things only restrict our freedom, keeping us ensnared in misperception.

This is why it's so important to let go of everything before drawing our final earthly breath. If we don't, we'll find ourselves hooked into returning to the three-dimensional plane, where again we will labor to transmute old karmic debts.

At the moment of death, we must be free of all attachments, whether of desire or loathing. Only in this way can we walk directly into the light without turning back, becoming salt statues.

If we were to change our concept of this life and view it not as the only and most important one, but rather as one more stage in our long process of evolution, we would better understand the true meaning of what is meant by death.

About the Authors

Carmen de Sayve is a Mexican psychic and author.

Thanks to her mediumship and extra sensory faculties she has written several books based on the teachings she receives from higher dimension masters.

Through her capabilities, she provides help to those who, after death, find themselves lost or in a difficult transition due to their attachments to the material world and their limiting beliefs. She helps them to clarify their beliefs that keep them stuck in the low astral world so that they can see the light of heaven. At the same time she brings comfort to the bereaved. She gives lectures and conferences on these subjects.

Speaker and channeler **Jocelyn Arellano** is a professional researcher in the field of the soul's evolutionary process in the third dimension and fourth dimension which includes life on planet Earth and on the different stages in the Astral world. She also sheds light on how our lives on earth have a direct impact on how we will experience the other side. At the same time she brings depth into how the shift in consciousness that this planet is undergoing affects our daily experience bringing exceptional opportunities for the soul's opening into higher frequencies.